T0207668

A
DANGEROUS
FAITH

Counting the Cost of a Life for Christ

Chris Byers

WESTBOW
PRESS®
A DIVISION OF THOMAS NELSON
& ZONDERVAN

WestBow Press books may be ordered through booksellers or by contacting:

WestBow Press
A Division of Thomas Nelson & Zondervan
1663 Liberty Drive
Bloomington, IN 47403
www.westbowpress.com
844-714-3454

Because of the dynamic nature of the Internet, any web addresses or links contained in this book may have changed since publication and may no longer be valid. The views expressed in this work are solely those of the author and do not necessarily reflect the views of the publisher, and the publisher hereby disclaims any responsibility for them.

Any people depicted in stock imagery provided by Getty Images are models, and such images are being used for illustrative purposes only. Certain stock imagery © Getty Images.

"Scripture quotations are from the ESV® Bible (The Holy Bible, English Standard Version®), copyright © 2001 by Crossway, a publishing ministry of Good News Publishers. Used by permission. All rights reserved."

Scripture quotations taken from The Holy Bible, New International Version® NIV® Copyright © 1973 1978 1984 2011 by Biblica, Inc. TM. Used by permission. All rights reserved worldwide.

Scripture taken from the King James Version of the Bible.

"Scripture taken from the NEW AMERICAN STANDARD BIBLE®, Copyright © 1960,1962,1963,1968,1971,1972,1973,1975,1977,1995 by The Lockman Foundation. Used by permission. www.Lockman.org"

ISBN: 978-1-6642-1303-6 (sc)
ISBN: 978-1-6642-1302-9 (hc)
ISBN: 978-1-6642-1304-3 (e)

Library of Congress Control Number: 2020922824

Print information available on the last page.

WestBow Press rev. date: 12/23/2020

To my wife, Juliet, and daughter, Hannah, my greatest blessings. In memory of my mom, LeeAnn Swanson, who inspired my love of writing.

Contents

Preface

SOME MAY WONDER WHY I CHOSE TO USE A TERM SUCH AS *DANGER* regarding the Christian faith. Though the concept came quickly to my mind, the essence of it has been churning within for many years now. As I looked around at the world and my brethren within the church, I realized there was a problem. I looked at myself and where I had come from and noticed the same problem. We have become a culture of Christians in name alone. I thought about some reasons as to why this might be the case and decided it must be, at least partially, because fully committing to Christ in word and deed requires an acceptance of the many dangers inherent to Christ's call.

It is important to note that not everyone looking at the faith, or already within the faith, will struggle with each of the dangers mentioned. For some, maybe only one or two will stand out. It is my hope for those who do not fall into some of these, that they become a help to other believers who may struggle. For example, I have no issue discerning false doctrine, but perhaps another brother or sister is confused about his or her beliefs. It would be wise of me to help them through this struggle, to reach the safety of sound doctrine. I do not believe doctrine is a bad word when used regarding the essential truths of our faith.

These notions compelled me to write this book. I do not wish to make it a book on how to be a legalistic Christian. Rather, I want it to cause all of us, whether those curious about the faith or in it for years, to take a step back and look at what Christ required of those who would call themselves His followers. The cost is high, but the reward is greater. Endurance and perseverance are key, and true commitment is required.

As we assess the dangers of the faith, I hope it provides a framework for how to follow Christ in relative safety. Yes, some of these dangers cannot be avoided. But for the dangers that would easily cause us to stray, I hope in writing this, I will prevent my brothers and sisters in Christ from so easily compromising with the world. We will examine everything from false gospels and views of Christ to the possibility of giving our lives for Christ.

I have arranged the dangers alphabetically, but that does not reflect any ranking otherwise. Throughout the spectrum, let all of the dangers be equally serious in their discussion, but realize some are dangerous in different ways than others. We will conclude by discussing how we can overcome these dangers and our future hope as Christians that propels us onward through a faith inherently costly to those who would believe. I pray it will be a help to you.

The Danger of Backsliding

WHEN WE THINK OF THE DANGERS OF THE CHRISTIAN FAITH, IT IS important to specifically address a danger to which all Christians, whether new or mature in the faith, can be susceptible. That is the danger of backsliding (regressing) back into our old sinful habits and ways of living.

I find this to be one of the most difficult dangers to overcome because we are always subject to temptation. Even Christ was subjected to temptation, though He at least did not give in or sin:

> For we do not have a high priest [Christ] who is unable to empathize with our weaknesses, but we have one who has been tempted in every way, just as we are— yet he did not sin. (Hebrews 4:15 NIV)

Those who are in Christ need not feel alone when we are tempted or fall back into weakness. Unlike Christ, the expectation of the curse of sin in the world is that we will still fall at times. We cannot achieve perfect righteousness on our own, but Christ's death on the cross is representative of the fact that for Christians, our penalty for sin— past, present, and future—has been paid. This is good news indeed!

> God made him who had no sin to be sin for us, so that in him we might become the righteousness of God. (2 Corinthians 5:21 NIV)

Since we are covered by Christ's atoning sacrifice for our sin, and we can confess and repent for forgiveness, why is backsliding to sin a problem? Could we not just pray our way back to God's good graces, knowing Christ's sacrifice will cover our multitude of sins? Paul speaks to this directly in his letter to the Romans:

> What shall we say then? Are we to continue in sin that grace may abound? By no means! How can we who died to sin live in it? (Romans 6:1–2)

Paul goes on to speak about our baptism into Christ's death. He says that our old selves were crucified with Christ at our conversion (v. 6) so that we do not remain slaves to our sins. The concept is presented clearly, but for many Christians, our humanity still has a way of sneaking back and tempting us to regress into the same sins.

To better understand the practical implications to believers, let us look at some specific struggles and what consequences a regression after conversion can have on us. I struggled with a temptation to view things I should not view on the internet for a good part of my adult life. Though I consider myself saved and renewed in Christ, I can say firsthand that the struggle of temptation on Christians in their lives is very real. Yet, the Bible tells us:

> Therefore, if anyone is in Christ, he is a new creation. The old has passed away; behold, the new has come. (2 Corinthians 5:17)

The expectation then is that, in Christ, we are not our old selves. However, as great as it would be to achieve perfection upon believing in Christ, we are still new creations living in sinful dwellings. Our hearts may be turned to righteousness in a spiritual sense, but our physical dwellings are still subjected to the curse of sin. Before speaking of us as new creations, in verse 15 of the same chapter, Paul says that Christ died for all so that we might not live now for ourselves but for the sake of Christ (2 Corinthians 5:15).

Though falling into sin after becoming believers does not negate our salvation, there are still consequences for those wishing to grow and mature in their relationship with Christ. Let us briefly explore three potential consequences that can come about for believers who yield to temptation. The danger of backsliding comes with the potential consequences of a damaged witness, physical and emotional damages, and loss of confidence or assurance in our salvation.

Damaged Witness

The first consequence that can occur is a *damaged witness*. Christ has called us to make disciples and to bring the Gospel to the world. But how can we be lights of Christ to the world if we are still stuck in the darkness of our sin?

> And he said to them, "Go into all the world and proclaim the Gospel to the whole creation." (Mark 16:15)

Regression can make it difficult for Christians to be used by God for their true purpose. I have learned this firsthand during times in my life when I have fallen back to temptation. Opportunities to be in God's will and to grow in the kingdom were removed or readjusted. Christians believe that being in the will of God and being used for His purpose is the primary desire of this life. However, backsliding into sin can often derail or delay God's plans for us. Likely, we have also seen instances in the headlines of pastors or church leaders falling into sin, which becomes public and damages their witness—and, usually, Christianity as a whole along with it. This goes along with what we'll speak about next.

Relational Troubles

Other consequences of backsliding into sin are the physical and emotional damages it can create. Relationships are a prime area where the consequences of sin can manifest. For example, alcoholics who regress into heavy drinking after being saved can see physical consequences show up within their bodies as well as difficulties within relationships that were renewed when they first stopped drinking. Sin can make us revert to old lifestyles that were damaging to ourselves and others. Marriages and friendships can be directly affected and scarred by the believer's regression into sin.

At this point, I should again clarify that once we are in Christ and have been born again into His kingdom, the fall back into temptation will not cause a loss of our salvation. The consequences may be hurtful and many, but if we are truly in Christ, nothing will remove us from that grace. I say if we are truly in Christ because if we do find ourselves constantly sinning after our conversion, we need to assess that it was a true conversion. We should always seek to work out our salvation and be sure we are in the faith.

> Therefore, my beloved, as you have always obeyed, so now, not only as in my presence but much more in my absence, work out your own salvation with fear and trembling. (Philippians 2:12)

> Examine yourselves, to see whether you are in the faith. Test yourselves. Or do you not realize this about yourselves, that Jesus Christ is in you? —unless indeed you fail to meet the test! (2 Corinthians 13:5)

Questioning Our Assurance of Salvation

Regression can damage our assurance of salvation and lead us to doubt as we wonder if we can truly be saved since we continually fall back into sin. This has been the biggest consequence that I have experienced as a product of sinful behaviors, and it has been spiritually and emotionally damaging. Faith is a major aspect of the Christian walk, and doubt and fear can directly affect the true faith of believers. This may lead to questioning whether or not they are true Christians in the first place.

Though I understand my assurance confidently now, at times in my life, this has been the biggest struggle. And I know it was a product of yielding to temptations that arose. However, I can say that if we are in Christ, we know that we can be forgiven and cleansed from unrighteous behaviors. His Word says we will never be tempted beyond what we can endure.

> If we confess our sins, he [Christ] is faithful and just to forgive our sins and to cleanse us from all unrighteousness. (1 John 1:9)

> No temptation has overtaken you that is not common to man. God is faithful, and he will not let you be tempted beyond your ability, but with the temptation he will also provide the way of escape, that you may be able to endure it. (1 Corinthians 10:13)

And though we know God is not the author of temptation (James 1:13–14), Paul seems to say that even in temptation authored by Satan or ourselves, God always provides a way out.

Despite knowing all of this, for Christians who sin, it is easy to begin to question their salvation. And in not trusting our salvation—as long as we truly believe what we say we believe—we lessen Christ's sacrifice.

As we look back then to the consequences of sin as believers, we can see it has affected our relationships with people and manifested in our relationship with Christ. The consequences, though no longer damning to us in a salvation sense, can seriously jeopardize our relational growth in the faith.

We will not be without sin in this life, but we must still choose to avoid what can lead us back into perpetual sin. Also, we must not use grace as a license to sin. The writer of Hebrews presents the assurance of our ongoing faith by Christ's atonement but also warns of the danger of continuing to sin after becoming a believer:

> Therefore, brothers, since we have confidence to enter the holy places by the blood of Jesus … let us draw near with a true heart in full assurance of faith, with our hearts sprinkled clean from an evil conscience and our bodies washed with pure water. (Hebrews 10:19, 22)

The assurance is always there. Christ will not lose those whom God has called by His Holy Spirit. Assurance should not be the worry of a believer. However, when we fall into patterns of sin, as the writer of Hebrews points out, we begin to see doubt of that assurance, and consequently, we become less effective in the faith. The following verses can give us comfort and insight into this truth:

> For if we go on sinning deliberately after receiving the knowledge of the truth, there no longer remains a sacrifice for sins, but a fearful expectation of judgment. (Hebrews 10:26–27)

> All that the Father gives me will come to me, and whoever comes to me I will never cast out. (John 6:37)

> My sheep hear my voice, and I know them, and they follow me. I give them eternal life, and they will never perish, and no one will snatch them out of my hand. My Father, who has given them to me, is greater than all, and no one is able to snatch them out of the Father's hand. I and the Father are one. (John 10:27–30)

> Who saved us and called us to a holy calling, not because of our works but because of his own purpose

and grace, which he [God] gave us in Christ Jesus
before the ages began. (2 Timothy 1:9)

In Hebrews 10:26 specifically, the writer is not saying that Christ's
sacrifice for our sin is negated if we sin. He is saying that the focus
will be on fear of judgment and doubt instead of on the atoning
sacrifice of Christ. Having gone through this valley myself, I can
say this is true. At my lowest times, amid sin patterns, the fear of
judgment and doubt of my assurance took away the focus of growing
in my walk with Christ.

When we give in to temptation and sin as Christians, we can
easily fall back into a pattern of sinning. Though Christ is still
faithful to forgive us, we must not use God's grace as an excuse to
sin. We should have full confidence in our salvation and Christ's
sacrifice for us. And we should avoid sin, which will cause doubt to
enter our minds—and often cause relational issues with loved ones
and with Christ.

When we do fall, we must confess and repent so that we may
be forgiven. This repentance is more relational for believers since
Christ's atonement has technically covered all of our sins. Christians
who truly believe in Christ will feel the guilt and shame of falling
back into a pattern of sinful behavior. The Holy Spirit will convict
and bring us to repentance. This is also the assurance of our salvation.
To recognize our failings as Christians, and to seek to be back in
God's grace, is a manifestation of the influence of the Holy Spirit in
our lives and of our faith in Christ.

When the woman was caught in adultery and was to be stoned,
Christ, in grace, did not condemn her. But He cautioned her to "go, and
sin no more" (John 8:11 KJV). Let us take comfort in the fact that once
we are in Christ, the old nature has passed away. We can overcome
the temptation to sin, and we can lean fully on Christ to lead us out
of temptation. Let us not lose our assurance but confidently know our
place in Christ. In doing so, we allow God to use us to our full abilities,
and our part in His worthy plan will come to fruition, unencumbered
by our failings and renewed by the grace found in Christ.

Overcoming the Danger of Backsliding

Overcoming this danger involves first acknowledging there is a sin problem—or that we have been using our grace in Christ as a license to sin. Practically, we can also begin to identify triggers that may be leading us into patterns of sin. Alcoholics should not tempt themselves by having a beer with dinner. Christians who struggle with pornography should watch what entertainment they view and which web pages they frequent. Avoiding these trigger situations can be a great step forward in overcoming our sin patterns.

Most important, however, is spending time with God. Reading the Bible, studying, and growing in the knowledge of our Savior removes desires and temptations that would conflict with His will for our lives. If we are to be distracted by something, let us be distracted by a hunger for God. Though we all will struggle at times, I've found in my most serious times of temptation, opening the Bible—or simply praying and taking a step back from the situation—is a surefire way to avoid sin. Alternatively, we could find another brother or sister in Christ who can help relate to our struggles and serve as a means of accountability.

As with most of the dangers inherent to the Christian faith, the more we mature in our walks with Christ—and the deeper we enter into our relationship with God—generally, the less we will struggle with this type of danger.

The Danger of Complacency

LIKE MANY OF US, I GREW UP ATTENDING CHURCH. SUNDAY SERVICE was another expectation of the week. And attending church was seen as a positive thing. But by the time I graduated high school and reflected back on my time in our home church, I could not detect much actual Christian growth in myself. Sure, I had good times and made friends, but I'd be hard-pressed to recall an encouraging sermon or explain what being saved meant at that point.

It wasn't that we didn't have Bible-believing Christians in the church; it was just that it had become another social activity. I grew complacent in my walk and looked forward more to playing games and trying to get attention from girls who were out of my league than a devotional or the Bible. I'm sure some of this can be blamed on teenage attention span and maturity, but when I attended my first nondenominational church in college, I heard a sermon on salvation the first day and immediately knew more about my faith than I had learned in all of those years attending my home church. Looking back, I knew people who attended churches in town that talked about salvation and Christ, and those teenagers understood their walks with Christ. That was not my experience—nor was it the experience, I'm sure, of many who grew up in my same position.

When parents raise their children in a Christian environment, it can strengthen the children's resolve to follow Christ even into adulthood. And deep down, something was brewing in me that just hadn't clicked until I got out of my hometown and into a new environment. However, there is a dangerous trend in which simply attending a service once a week gives people the impression that they are Christians. Sadly, many go years without ever truly believing in Christ, yet they think they are saved because they attended church each week or were baptized as children. For those who are truly in Christ, there is still a danger of becoming complacent in our spiritual growth when church is just a box that we check off of our lists each week. I like to say, "A butt in the pew does not a Christian make."

As Christians, we are saved by grace, not works. The fellowship with other believers at church is important, but we should not treat going to church as equal to salvation in Christ. This danger of the faith is in identifying with church attendance or a denomination as a measure of salvation. Christians have a tendency to become complacent when Sunday services become just another routine.

In the first years after Christ's death, when Christianity was being formed by the disciples and followers of Jesus, the church was simply the body of believers. In truth, Christ's bride, the church, is the body of believers and not the building in which they gather. The early church met in the homes of fellow believers, not necessarily the grand, ornate buildings we associate with the word church today.

Fellowship has always been an important aspect of the faith. In the early church, it was a necessity. The survival of Christianity in its early days was dependent upon believers coming together to worship and clarify their beliefs. In the present day, with estimates of tens of thousands of denominations and sects of Christianity worldwide, it is easy to lose sight of the Gospel and the reason believers gather together. Encouragement in our struggles and discernment are just two of many reasons that attending a church is still important.

Some believers, in an effort to focus on Christ alone, have taken to individualizing their Christianity and cutting out traditional worship. While a focus on Christ is never bad, these believers alienate themselves from Gospel-focused preaching and the support of fellow believers. As I mentioned in the "Danger of Backsliding," even the strongest Christians are tempted at times, and when we individualize our faith, there is no support of the church body when struggles come. I have found in my experience that nothing can encourage and renew our spirits like fellowship with other believers. The idea of our personal relationship with Christ should not lead us to neglect the body of Christ as a whole. And the church, as it should be, is His body.

Fellowship and Salvation

When we first commit our lives to Christ, we are transformed. However, we must still work out our salvation daily in earnest. This process is known as sanctification, and sanctification is ongoing. We may have an altar call conversion or accept Christ alone in our rooms. Whatever the means, though, we are justified in a moment—and we must be sanctified throughout our lives. So, what does this process of sanctification look like?

> Therefore, my beloved, as you have always obeyed, so now, not only as in my presence but much more in my absence, work out your own salvation with fear and trembling. (Philippians 2:12)

In one sense, it is the daily striving to live our new lives in Christ, functioning in a state that is more like Christ than our previous mindset. This could mean breaking existing addictions or seeking God more avidly. We commit ourselves to Christ and then live daily for Him. We let our lights shine to a dark world, and we are set apart.

We may not be perfect at our moment of conversion, but we must strive ever after to lead lives in pursuit of Christ. Though we won't attain perfection in this life, we are made whole in His grace and forgiveness. We may still fail rarely or often, depending on the challenges faced by each person, but our contrite hearts in repenting to Christ draw us ever back to His righteousness. We are not dead in our sins because of grace, but as mentioned previously, we do not use grace as an excuse to go on sinning.

If we are honest, a complacent believer is in sin. While an apathetic attitude or lack of growth may not seem as heinous as other sins, they can eat away at the heart just as ravenously. We should grow in Christ from the time of our conversion and not remain complacent or the same as we were before. We are to be a new creation, the old passed away (2 Corinthians 5:17). The apostle Paul, for example, experienced frustration with a lack of growth within the Corinthian church:

> But I, brothers, could not address you as spiritual people, but as people of the flesh, as infants in Christ. I fed you with milk, not solid food, for you were not ready for it. And even now you are not ready, for you are still of the flesh. (1 Corinthians 3:1–3)

Paul addresses the improper behavior of the young Corinthian church multiple times in his first letter to them. They were a church converted in Christ, but they were lacking much substance or growth in Christ. That is a danger we still face today in the church—in all sects and denominations of Christianity.

Part of the problem can occur when leadership in a church begins to desire numbers over saints. In an effort to get everyone in the doors, often, the task of discipling new converts falls by the wayside. They are converted, but they don't know where to go from there. Many continue living as before and often cause their views, however un-Christian, to seep into the body. It is this which is at least partially responsible for the invasion of secular culture and beliefs into our modern churches.

Paul also says, "A little leaven leavens the whole lump" (Galatians 5:9). That is, individuals in the church can have a direct impact on the body as a whole, and behaviors or beliefs that do not align with Christianity have the power to spread throughout the body, eating away at it and creating instances of division or deception.

It isn't a bad thing to have a large church, but elders of churches with too many people to individually know need strong leaders in place to disciple and grow the congregation, especially the recently converted. This can be a problem in smaller churches as well.

Sometimes people are so comfortable in church and routine that they stop growing and let the church grow stagnant.

Many denominations have seen this problem as families of longtime members in the church refuse change and growth in favor of familiarity and comfort. With no growth allowed, the members stay happily complacent while their beliefs shift back to the world and not Christ.

Churches allowing people who are knowingly in sin without remorse into leadership may be another product of the general complacency of American Christian churches. Pastors and leaders are more interested in keeping everyone happy and comfortable than in creating actual disciples of the Gospel. This allows much Gospel truth to be set aside in favor of pleasing everyone who walks in the door to boost membership numbers and maintain cohesion with the cultural status quo. Meanwhile, the members continue to be fed milk, not meat (see 1 Corinthians 3:1–3 above) because it is easier to be a babe in the faith than to reach for actual sanctification and growth.

The danger of complacency is real for both elders and congregants of the church. While getting people to church for fellowship and growth is important to Christians, the flip side is that we must be experiencing this fellowship in a church that cares to grow disciples in Christ and not just add rear ends to the seats.

Denomination Over Salvation

Another by-product of the tendency of complacency in the church is the identification of oneself by denomination alone. To pick on them a bit, this seems most common to those within the Catholic Church. That is people essentially thinking that by identifying as Catholic and going to Mass, they are saved or have a relationship with Christ. While it is true that many people who identify as Catholics may believe in Christ for salvation, many others may not even grasp this idea.

Honestly, it's not just Catholics. Anywhere you have a mainline

Christian denomination, there will be people who identify more in name than in actual saving grace. They'll say things like, "I'm a good Catholic," or "I'm a good Baptist," but they often have put their faith in the denomination instead of Christ. Denomination association as a replacement for salvation is an inherent danger of the faith. The early church simply followed the teachings of Christ. The various sects did not come about all at once.

Many Christian denominations preach the true Gospel of Christ and simply differ in style of worship. Some favor more traditional services, and others like a more modern service. As long as the Gospel is not distorted in these variations, we have nothing about which to be concerned. However, when churches are so traditional that they become legalistic, or so modern that they begin to cherry-pick the Gospel to be more culturally accommodating, we have a danger of putting our denominations over salvation. Christ is our only means of salvation (Acts 4:11–12; John 14:6), and a denomination that forgets this simple fact is headed down a dangerous path.

In Mexico, where my wife is originally from, many sects of Catholicism have taken up the former saints of the faith as idols. Some American Catholics have done this to a degree as well. The reverence for Mary, the mother of Jesus, can often border on worship. Though she was the vessel chosen to bring Christ into the world, she is not a savior herself—and certainly not an object of worship.

Many gang members also identify with a denomination or sect of the Christian faith, yet they do not have a problem killing or creating havoc on a daily basis. They simply pray to their patron saint and go on with their lives. Others wear crosses as jewelry but have no intention of following Christ. This denominational identification without true repentance for sin is a false salvation. It is simply religion without Christ. The atonement and resurrection of Christ are what make Him the unique religious figure, but salvation in Christ is more about a relationship with Him than religious identification.

When we identify only by denomination, we get complacent. If I think I'm a good Baptist, Catholic, or other mainline denomination, why bother with Christian growth and sanctification? Maybe I tithe my 10 percent, attend my service, and go about my business. Treating the church as an obligation instead of attending for knowledge and growth can easily lead to complacent attitudes. And on the extreme end, it can lead some Christians to lose sight of the Gospel's exclusiveness in Christ. If we make Christianity another religion of works or obligation, we loop it in with all the other work-based religions out there.

The exclusivity of Christ and His oneness with God are precisely the gospel truths that other religions are missing. He is our salvation, the only atoning sacrifice that can redeem us from our sinful nature:

> And there is salvation in no one else, for there is no other name under heaven given among men by which we must be saved. (Acts 4:12)

> Jesus said to him, "I am the way, and the truth, and the life. No one comes to the Father except through me." (John 14:6)

Because of this and the importance of the Gospel being shared to the ends of the earth, we need Christians who seek to be like Christ and not those who simply want to meet a sense of weekly obligation or confession to men for repentance instead of to Christ.

When Paul says to work out salvation with "fear and trembling" (Philippians 2:12), there is an implication of something challenging. I refer to this verse frequently because it is essential that we treat our salvation as a serious matter and seek growth in our walks. Simply checking the church service off of our to-do lists every week does not promote growth within the faith.

If we are truly saved and converted in Christ, we seek to live daily for Him. The Christians who are in this position see church services as a chance to experience fellowship and get help with struggles and not as a to-do item. Those who simply associate with a denomination, or attend out of obligation, are victims of the danger of complacency in the Christian faith.

Once we are fully renewed in Christ, our next calling is to spread the Word to the rest of the world. This evangelism is not just a suggestion; it is a biblical requirement for Christians. We might prefer to gloss over this—I'll admit even I have had trouble making the move toward this in my walk—but it is something we cannot ignore.

Evangelism and the Christian Walk

Over the years, I've learned that evangelism and spreading the Gospel might not look the same for everyone. My mentality, which often hindered me, was that I needed to be out on a street corner yelling at people for Jesus to be considered good at fulfilling the Great Commission. However, I've come to realize that service, in general, is the beginning of evangelism.

The world will primarily see Christians by their actions, and while these actions do not in any way save us from sin, they are a product of a new life in Christ. When we look at the danger of complacency, what is making everyone so complacent? Why are the churches not growing disciples? I'm beginning to have some idea as time goes by, though I certainly do not have all of the answers.

I'll speak to what has caused me to fall into complacency at times: a lack of purpose.

My maternal grandmother was a great example of fulfilling her God-given purpose and running the race of faith to completion. Late in her life, God put it on her heart to create a place where all who wanted to sing for the Lord could come and perform, regardless of abilities. Her "Sonshine Gospel Singing Barn" became her purpose, and she used it for many years to glorify God.

My grandpa also responded to God's call in this by doing everything he could to make sure her gospel barn became a reality. Gospel singers locally, and later from all over the country, came out on the third Saturday every month for many years to sing to the Lord. Even when diagnosed with aggressive cancer, God sustained her longer than the doctors expected so that she could continue the work for Him here on earth. When her time finally came, she went on to glory having fulfilled her purpose for God, and she no doubt heard, "Well done, good and faithful servant," when she closed her eyes and entered into her Savior's arms.

We are put on this earth to glorify God using the gifts and talents that he has bestowed upon us. When we realize that the ultimate goal of the Christian walk is not just buying our ticket to heaven but in achieving our God-given purpose in this life as well, we begin to have something motivating to work toward.

I must again emphasize that this working toward purpose is not in any way saying that by doing better at seeking our calling, we are saving ourselves by works. This is speaking to the sanctification of the believer. Again, that is the daily walk with Christ and maturing in the faith that comes as a product and a requirement of justification in the moment of conversion.

If we truly assess our gifts and abilities, it's easy to get a general idea of what we can do well. Some are skilled builders, some are musicians, and some are good at learning languages. Others may be teachers, writers, or pastors. Being in ministry does not automatically mean we have to be the lead pastor of a church. When we realize what we can contribute, the church begins to see growth. Then outreach and service, which ultimately lead to evangelism and sharing the Gospel, can take place in a very natural way.

I speak to this more at this stage of my life because we have ultimately found a church in our hometown that fully embraces this concept. They are doing great things for the community—while still training up believers who are truly saved and desiring to grow in their walks with Christ. Our pastor encourages us to use our gifts and talents for outreach and within the church body. Some are good with technical things, and perhaps they run media on Sundays. Some own companies that can provide a product or service for families in need. We can all contribute in some way.

This contribution and working toward our purposes, with other believers engaged in doing the same, naturally leads to fellowship and growth in our walks. There is no avoiding it. There are motivation and support, and there are training and teaching during the week to help encourage us and redirect us back to the reason we do any of it.

Evangelism may sometimes be standing on a street corner handing out pamphlets or spontaneously praying for someone we meet, but it can just as easily be coordinated activities for outreach, mission trips, community engagement, or simple service within the church. Serving actively in a church gets our mind set for the week and keeps us engaged with other believers throughout the week. We make friends who are trying to grow just as we are, and we grow together in faith and fellowship. Meanwhile, our hearts incline more toward Christ, and our faith matures. This also leads to more opportunity for evangelism, either by how we are perceived in daily life—people always watch the actions of a Christian—or perhaps in telling someone about Christ now that we have learned to better express our faith.

Overcoming the Danger of Complacency

How do we overcome the danger of complacency? We understand that though we are saved in an instant, we are running a marathon for Christ. The writer of Hebrews says those who have gone before us are cheering for us (Hebrews 12:1).

When church and God are just checkmarks on our to-do lists, even if we are truly saved, it becomes very easy to get apathetic or complacent. And finding a church home that challenges us to grow in our walks with Christ is a necessary factor as well. I don't encourage "church hopping," but I do believe if we are in a church in which no growth is occurring, we should find a good Bible-believing church that provides opportunities to serve and become involved. It doesn't always have to be as a pastor or a worship team member; there are hundreds of ways someone can use a talent for the kingdom, probably more.

Let this encourage us to wake up and get to work on discovering and fulfilling our purposes in Christ. We need to spend time in the

Word and prayer and grow in our knowledge of Christ. For new believers, find a mature, Bible-believing Christian who can help mentor and grow you in the faith as well.

Pastors on Sunday are a huge component, but what happens during the week in our daily lives is even more important. That's when the world is watching. Do we want to identify with a denomination to acknowledge that we sat in the pew again last Sunday, but we don't recall anything the preacher said? Or do we want to be telling people about the next great outreach event or about how God is using our skills and gifts to help others within the church and outside its walls?

We are still not saved by our works, but we are called to bear fruit in our Christian walks. Let us pray for God to reveal His purpose to us and be ready when He does. It may be one thing or multiple things, but we have all been blessed and gifted with something that can better the kingdom. Then we can quit thinking of church as a to-do list item and get out there to glorify God.

The Danger of Compromise

Do not be conformed to this world, but be transformed by the renewal of your mind, that by testing you may discern what is the will of God, what is good and acceptable and perfect. (Romans 12:2)

YEAR BY YEAR, CULTURAL NORMS ARE REDEFINED. ACCEPTANCE OF things not previously accepted becomes the new normal. With social media, we become exposed to these changes on an almost daily basis. For the discerning Christian, many of these new cultural norms stretch further and further away from biblical truth. At that point, Christians begin to experience the "danger of compromise." They begin the inner struggle of choosing to stand on biblical truths or bending to the will of the culture.

When Christ said the world would hate His followers, we get a clear picture that Christians will not—and really should not—be aligned with the culture on many things. Though some changes can be good, a large chunk can draw us away from our focus on the Bible's teachings. On topics of money, church attendance, and biblical authority, the culture is not in standing with the Bible. Let's address these in a bit more detail to help clarify and ultimately learn how to avoid a compromise of our faith with the culture.

Money

The world economy says we should all be making as much money as possible. Commercials and advertisements further emphasize this with enticing new "toys" and things that we must have if we are to be considered successful. To some degree, this is okay. For example, having internet access and a device to use for accessing it has become a necessity in our modern world—and churches have utilized this tool (mostly) for good. Expanding the Gospel's reach is another benefit. Christians across the world now have a means of reaching one another.

On the other hand, a constant emphasis on having the latest and greatest items means we begin to think in more covetous ways. We focus on what we want to have instead of being content with what we do have. Paul discusses this plainly on various occasions:

> Not that I am speaking of being in need, for I have learned in whatever situation I am to be content … In any and every circumstance, I have learned the secret of facing plenty and hunger, abundance and need. I can do all things through him who strengthens me. (Philippians 4:11–13)

> For we brought nothing into the world, and we cannot take anything out of the world. But if we have food and clothing, with these we will be content.

> (1 Timothy 6:7–8)

Peter Anderson wrote "10 Bible Verses About Contentment: How Can We Feel Contentment in a Restless World?"

> Many of us are trying to fill a void … with things that can't satisfy. We look to fill it with possessions or money, but only end up craving more. These things

aren't necessarily bad things, but when they become the end goals, we end up being discontent since these things were never meant to fill us.[1]

As Paul mentioned in his letter to the Philippians, he has learned to be content in whatever situation because of his reliance on Christ. He reminds Timothy that we cannot take anything with us when we leave this world. Godly contentment is the Bible's goal for us.

Juliet and I have learned in our years of marriage that ultimately seeking possessions can only lead to more trouble. I've long ago forgotten what we bought with our credit cards—even though we're still paying the balances on many of them. The temptation to just charge now to get what we want is strong. At the end of the day, whether we have extra money in the bank or zero dollars, we must learn to be content in Christ and not in money.

Biblically, one important means of getting our finances on track as Christians can seem like an obvious one, yet it is often overlooked. I am referring to tithing. I used to argue in college that New Covenant believers were not commanded to tithe—or at least not the 10 percent of the Old Covenant. It was ultimately an attempt to justify keeping more for myself, probably to buy more DVDs at the time. (My collection in college was pushing five hundred.) I also reasoned that it was more important to have that money "just in case." Even into married life, I maintained this idea. If tithing meant we would have less money for groceries or that "extra" so often desired, then God would certainly prefer we have that for ourselves. What we eventually learned, though, is that the giving of a tithe is less about money—God obviously doesn't need our money—than it is a true act of faith in action.

Even well-meaning Christians often guard their money in a more worldly fashion. We never want to go without it. Or we adopt the "I

---

[1] Anderson, Peter. "10 Bible Verses About Contentment: How Can We Feel Contentment in a Restless World." Bible Money Matters. October 25, 2018. https://www.biblemoneymatters.com/10-bible-verses-about-contentment-how-can-we-feel-contentment-in-a-restless-world/.

work hard for my money" mind-set. By letting go of a portion of something so precious to God first, we say, "I trust you to provide, Lord. I lean on God, not my money." So, 10 percent off the top is a great practice, and I can tell you even when the bank account dwindles and we lament not having our "extra," God always provides enough. Though it may not rain down from the skies, God does open the storehouses for us.

"Don't neglect the tithe" is the first piece of Christian financial advice I would offer to a new believer, having learned the hard way ourselves that keeping from God is a compromise with a culture that says everyone for themselves when it comes to finances. And this brings up another good aspect of Christianity versus culture—the cheerful giver.

> Each one must give as he has decided in his heart, not reluctantly or under compulsion, for God loves a cheerful giver. (2 Corinthians 9:7)

Paul's verse here really applies to our giving outside of the tithe. The tithe is the foundation stone of giving in God's economy. Giving above and beyond the tithe helps us move further into a biblical mind-set on financial matters.

Pastor Chad Large of Crosspointe Church in Ada, Oklahoma, compares our blessings from God to a river. God blesses us so that we can be a blessing. We are meant to give out of what we have, so like water flowing in a river, the blessing flows through us and out to others. If we block the river's flow, the blessing stops with us, and we become more like the culture. However, if we let the water of blessings flow, God will trust us with more—and continually bless and provide for us.[2]

"But, what about my bills and obligations?" we might say. We must still fulfill our obligations to the world in that it would be unwise to not pay our bills. Though God could provide us situations in which

---

[2] Large, Chad. "Go with the Flow." My Money Series: Week 1, 2018. https://crosspointeada.com/sermons/recorded-sermons/sermon-archives/my-money/.

we get a break, for the most part, bills are a part of life that we must accept. Let's look at a structure for God's economy that factors in our obligations to humanity and our faith toward God.

First, always, we tithe. Consider that 10 percent of everything brought in is already going to God. So, if you made $1,400, the first $140 of that is faithfully (and cheerfully) set apart to God. This would be the tithe to your church home, of which, ideally, practicing Christians will be a part.

From there, we pay our obligations. These would include things like rent, electricity, and internet. Once those are paid and essentials like food are accounted for, what is left is where we have the opportunity to implement God's economy of giving. Maybe, of that $1,400, we have $100 leftover. We can pray that God opens our eyes to needs around us, so that of the $100, perhaps we see a need to give or help out someone using a portion of it. Or we could even proactively set aside $20 and ask God to show us where that $20 (or more) can be used.

For Christians, we can expect that the Holy Spirit will convict us of the right time for this type of giving. Perhaps it is buying some gas or food for someone. Perhaps it is giving to a ministry other than your church home. And there are times when after all is said and done, we may not have anything left. That's okay. First, we still trust God's provision for us—even in lean seasons. Second, giving cheerfully doesn't have to be monetary. Maybe we have an old toy we don't use that someone else could use—or maybe we give our time to help someone. The overall pattern for God's economy, however, is tithing, obligations and needs, and extra giving.

For Juliet and me, in our leanest times, when there was nothing in the bank for the week, if we had faithfully tithed, God never let us down in providing something for us. Whether it was a family member proactively offering some money or a random refund check in the mail, we have been provided for when we put God first in our finances. We just have to get out of the cultural mind-set of more, more, more and into the godly mind-set of contentment with what God has provided. And as we are faithful with a little, God can begin to trust us with more. As the blessings then increase, we continue putting God first and are like a water hose that lets the blessings flow through us and out to others.

In contrast, the culture says, "Hold on to your money. You worked hard for it—enjoy it!" Though it is not "bad" in some sense to have some financial preparation for life (savings, 401(k), emergency fund), we must not let that be a higher focus than a giving spirit. And truthfully, it is hard. Please don't think because I write so easily about it, that it's easy to do. Like most things in the Christian walk, it takes discipline and developing a pattern of giving. And tithing doesn't suddenly drop money from the sky as prosperity preachers might lead us to believe. Though God "could" do that, more likely, He will test us a bit.

When we first began tithing diligently, we had a few instances of still having nothing in the bank. The temptation was to think, if we had the tithe money, we wouldn't have a zero-dollar balance. It tempted us to think that God's economy wasn't all that great. I speak more to it later in "The Danger of Doubt," but as a coach trains the team for a big game, God will train us. It may hurt a bit sometimes. As any athlete made to run laps can tell you, training is not always fun and painless, but the big picture is that we establish discipline and grow our faith and reliance on God, and thus our contentment in what He provides. We may not all be millionaires (sorry, this isn't that type of writing), but when we operate in God's economy, we will always become content and grow in our desire to give more than we receive. In doing so, we avoid the "danger of compromise" with our money.

Church Attendance

This compromise is more of an internal Christian compromise than one with the culture since the culture has no interest in church. However, it is a cultural compromise to some degree in that it has become a bit of a Christian subculture as more and more people become disenfranchised with traditional churches.

Over the years, most likely due to negative experiences in church, many professing Christians have adopted a "just me and Jesus" attitude. They see no need to attend church if they have that "personal" relationship with Jesus. And while it's true that God's church isn't limited to buildings and walls, Christians need the fellowship and accountability that comes from a church home. The writer of Hebrews says to not forsake the gathering together—as some do—but to meet and exhort one another, much more so as the day (Christ's return) comes near (Hebrews 10:25).

Some of the reasons for Christians skipping out on church are similar to why non-Christians steer clear. I address some of this in "The Danger of Hypocrisy" and "The Danger of Division." It boils down to seeing the church as just another place to meet our desires. Perhaps a Christian has a church home and attends regularly, but then one day, the band adds a drum set. Suddenly, it is more about the drums than any established church family. He or she reasons that if they just worship at home, or even hop down the road to a new church, their desires will be fulfilled. And so, in their minds, they are not doing anything wrong since they still have their personal relationship with Jesus. But my bet is if we took a poll of these individual nonchurchgoing Christians, all of that Jesus time they claim to get outside of the church would be much less than if they were to be active in a church home. One exception would be the need to avoid physical gatherings for health reasons. With the onset of COVID-19, it has become necessary in some cases to do only virtual church gatherings. There is nothing wrong with going that route, though ideally, we would still find ways to fellowship virtually through small groups or other activities that could be safely planned.

Christians need fellowship and the accountability of like-minded believers. We need mutual worship together of God. There isn't anything wrong with the online-sermon-at-home route once in a while, but really, we need the people within that church building. Admittedly, the churches have not always made this easy. So many churches have entered into a sleepy routine. There is no challenge to the people and no growth or attempt to help their sanctification. As we discussed in "The Danger of Complacency," in those churches, it is more like a weekly obligation. I feel for Christians raised in that type of church environment and can relate to them making a go of it on their own.

I learned more about salvation and faith when I got out of the church in which I grew up than I learned within it. However, I know that if we are truly seeking God, He will bring us to a church home where we can grow. Sometimes it is just for a season. We had a great home church in Austin that got Juliet and me back on fire in our faith, but then we moved away. God maintained the connections made there and led us to a new church home, and when the assistant pastor of that original church needed a worship leader for a church he was planting, I was on his short list.

The connections made with like-minded believers can lead us into opportunities to use our gifts for God and to grow in our sanctification so that we move forward in God's will for our lives. However, without church fellowship, these doors would never open. I'd be holed up at home, possibly learning but lacking that fellowship of other believers. Isolationist Christianity is a compromise. We need to pray that God opens our eyes to the church where He needs us to be. Since 2010, we've had three or four of these. We didn't leave any for petty reasons. God moved us as needed—as well as to always have a church family.

The Hebrew people craved being part of the assembly. Being out of it was considered punishment. Some may say Christ spoke against churches, but again, that isn't accurate. Jesus taught in the synagogues. His words against religion were directed at those who cared more for their traditions than for God and His people, which is like many churches today that are shrinking as they preach compromised messages that coddle the people instead of coaching them to mature. Other churches are hung up so much on traditions of the church itself—not biblical ones—that maintaining those is more important than teaching the Gospel. In those situations, it may be truly necessary for believers to get out and get somewhere they can grow. We cannot fully grow in isolation.

And beyond just committing to one day a week, we really should seek out ways to serve or meet with our church family throughout the week. A Sunday sermon will rarely keep our spiritual batteries fully charged during a workweek filled with stresses and opportunities to compromise with culture coming at us constantly. As Paul tells us in his letter to the Ephesians:

> In all circumstances take up the shield of faith, with which you can extinguish all the flaming darts of the evil one. (Ephesians 6:16)

Ultimately, church attendance is essential for avoiding the danger of compromise. When we surround ourselves with other believers who help us grow in our faith, we emerge stronger and more able to withstand cultural compromise during the week and during times when we are not at church.

Authority of Scripture

A few years ago, in the news, there was some controversy over a private Christian school using a curriculum from Ken Ham of the Answers in Genesis ministry.[3] His ministry focus is apologetics and education from a creation-based standpoint. The school came under attack because a quiz was given with answers corresponding to what the students had learned from one of Ken Ham's curriculum DVDs.

When some groups opposed to Ken's ministry found out about the school giving this quiz, there was a media firestorm. Atheists and even some Christians came out of the woodwork to condemn Mr. Ham and his ministry, and some even made threats toward the school itself. It turns out that to even suggest God could have created the world in six days instead of the evolutionary process is enough to get nonbelievers and even some believers riled. Through my research

---

[3] Ham, Ken. "Creation." Answers in Genesis, 2019, http://www.answersingenesis.org/creation.

into Ken's ministry, I would say everything they are teaching is scripturally based and accurate as it relates to God's Word. Mr. Ham understands salvation is found only in Christ and believes the essentials of the faith. Why is it then that so many are opposed to him, including many professing Christians?

I believe it has to do with a compromise of scriptural authority, in this case specifically on issues of creation. Ken Ham is not opposed to science as some would suggest. He simply understands that our Creator, God, who left us the Bible as His evidence, has also placed ample evidence within creation for us to understand His universe. Ken Ham simply approaches science from a perspective that places God's authority above the authority of humanity.

Belief in a young earth is not a salvation issue directly. Technically, we can believe in an old earth, and Jesus isn't going to revoke our salvation. However, it may reflect an authority issue, and that can be a slippery slope into other, more serious compromises. Not surprisingly, these days, there is a huge authority issue within the faith. People have left the Bible in favor of pop-culture Christianity that has Jesus floating around and telling everyone how great they are. It's not biblically sound, but it feeds the human desire to keep God out of the majority of our life decisions. And that is one of the most common areas to find that compromise with the world over God's Word.

Science is not incompatible with biblical thinking. There is no natural law or observation that God does not already fully control. We are told in chapter 1, verse 1 of God's Word that by His hand, all was created. And because He is God and can do this with no trouble, it was created in six days. There is no conflict with a six-day creation account for a professing Christian. We need only look to how God created and healed by the suspension of natural law throughout the Bible.

Considering Christ's miracles while on earth, for example, we can see that whenever God incarnate created or repaired something—as in the case of the blind gaining sight—the appearance of the finished product had all the markings of maturity of something that had existed in that state for a longer period of time. The ocular cavity and all parts of the eye, when the blind man gained sight, had the appearance of a healthy pair of eyes, despite only moments before having been damaged or unhealthy. Similarly, when Christ turned water into the complex fermented mixture that is a good wine, He created in an instant something with maturity it did not have moments before. The peptides and components of a wine, which Christ and the wedding guests said was a good-tasting actual wine, came together instantly with a word.

Paul tells us that Christ was the agent of the world's creation (Colossians 1:15–17). He is the second part of the Godhead. When we look to the biblical pattern of suspension of natural law, we can see that God is perfectly capable of forming a fully functioning, mature universe in six days. Not to mention, He created Adam and Eve as fully formed adults. If a scientist could travel back and examine them, he would determine that their bodies showed all of the expected evidence of humans who had grown from babies to adults. There is no need for a believer to compromise with the world's theories relating to age and the creation of our world. Our God creates with a word in an instant, and that which He creates always has the appearance of maturity and is a fully realized creation.

The world decided a few hundred years ago that if we didn't accept molecules to human evolution as cold, hard fact, we were idiots, crazy, or both. I can understand even today why those who do not believe in God would also think the same way. I still find it odd that Christians will willingly insult or battle other Christians based on this argument of scientific theory over scriptural authority. Scholars all over the world will attest to the validity of scripture. The book of Genesis account should stand firm in the face of scrutiny.

During our discussion of the authority of scripture, it would be helpful to address briefly how we understand scripture as the true, inerrant Word of God. It was laid out well in a sermon series I heard years ago from Brian Lightsey of Life Church in Leander, Texas. To paraphrase him a bit, the source of the Bible was God the Holy Spirit. The agent was human writers—sinful but still used by God—but the process was guided by the Holy Spirit. The result is inerrant and infallible scripture. Brian further broke it down into four I's: inspiration, illumination, interpretation, and implementation.

Inspiration is a supernatural act in which God, without overriding individual personality or literary style, directed human authors in the receiving and recording of divine truth in such a manner that what was written in the original manuscripts was without error, resulting in documents that are the very Word of God. Illumination is a supernatural act of God in which the Holy Spirit influences believers who are in right relationship with God to understand the Word of God. Interpretation is a supernatural act of observing the context (historical and literary) and content (grammar and words) to discover what it meant to early believers, so we can determine what it means to us. It cannot mean to us what it did not mean to them. Implementation is a supernatural act of letting the Word of God work in us so that we can apply it to our lives.[4] For more information on where we get the Bible and the evidence for it, I recommend the Origins of the Bible series by Mike Fabarez of Compass Bible Church and Focal Point Ministries. It is an in-depth look at the origins of this book that we call the Word of God and is a great tool for strengthening our knowledge of scripture and its trustworthiness.[5]

Compromising even on nonessentials for salvation can ultimately lead to other failings. If we can ignore God's authority in the very first words He gave to us, I would argue it's easier to compromise on other aspects of His Word. When talking about biblically sound, hard-to-take truths, sometimes people's feathers get ruffled. God's Word is a sharp sword, piercing and convicting to the heart, so it is no surprise things don't always sit well with everyone.

My word is not God's Word, but the Bible is God's Word—and I believe it. The grand drama of perfect creation, sin, the cross, and our eventual heavenly home is all based on the foundation that God

---

[4] Lightsey, Brian. "A Look at the Book." History: Part 1. June 9, 2013, https://yourlifechurch.org/sunday/sermons/?page=35.

[5] Fabarez, Mike. "Origins of the Bible." A Systematic Overview of Bibliology, 2009, https://focalpointministries.org/product/origins-of-the-bible-series/.

does what He says He does, did, and will do. I find that the scriptural story of creation is so tied into what Christ eventually did for us that believing it at face value strengthens my faith walk. Despite differing opinions on these issues, we all must recognize a sin problem and the need for Christ to eliminate that problem. It is the heart of the faith if the goal of our salvation and sanctification is to be ever more like Christ.

Overcoming the Danger of Compromise

The danger of compromise can occur in other ways than mentioned here, but some of the easiest cultural compromises to make for believers are with money, isolation in Christ, and accepting the world's views over the authority of God's Word. Regarding the topics here, when we trust the Lord in something big like finances, we will find it easier to trust Him in things like fulfilling His purpose for us in this life. And when we stand on the authority of the Word of God, even on the passages we are conditioned to find out of sync with the modern worldview, we can avoid compromise in other areas of our lives as well.

Though always present like the other dangers of the Christian walk, we can immerse ourselves in the Word of God and things of God to battle the temptation of compromise with a culture that is becoming increasingly hostile to Bible-believing Christians.

The Danger of Deception

THE DANGER OF DECEPTION IS A DANGER THAT IS VERY SPECIFIC TO Christians. Because of the exclusivity of Christ's claims, there are essential truths that must be accepted if we are to call ourselves Christ followers. Deception is not a danger for the world since it tends to believe everyone's truth is valid regardless of its alignment with the claims of Christ. The danger of deception can come in many forms, though two, in particular, come to mind. To avoid stumbling into this danger, especially as new believers, we must watch out for false gospels and false views of Christ that have the power to lead us astray:

> For false christs and false prophets will arise and perform great signs and wonders, so as to lead astray, if possible, even the elect. (Matthew 24:24)

False Gospels

I love to eat at Chinese buffet restaurants. There is just something about having all of that selection. I can take some chicken here, maybe some steak there, toss it all on a bed of fried rice, and I am one satisfied patron. Similarly, there are some areas of our lives as Christians where choice can be a good thing. There is one place, however, where Christians should not be looking for multiple-choice options. We cannot compromise the true Gospel message by making it into a buffet.

My favorite food is steak. Maybe a friend of mine decides his favorite food is spaghetti. We could argue all day back and forth about which is truly better because, ultimately, the answer is subjective. In this case, we might even say spaghetti is right for him, steak is right for me, and both of us need to accept one another's food decisions. In that context, it's perfectly fine. However, ultimate moral truth is not subjective. God's truth is not up for debate. We cannot take issues of subjective taste and apply them to truth claims as they relate to God. For Christians, any idea against the wisdom of God is wrong.

Some will see this as intolerant. Christ certainly expected those who follow to receive some guff for this. When He told us to take up our crosses and follow Him, He wasn't asking us to pick up fluffy pillows. Rather, He was telling us to pick up these representations of death and follow Him down the hard path ahead.

As Christians today in the United States, we often get so comfortable that we forget the real message of Christianity is not prosperity and riches for everyone. That isn't to say God could not grant us favor—in fact, He often does—but we must not forget the essential truth of the Gospel is that we are sinners, fallen from God's grace, and it is only by the cross of Christ, through His blood, that God's wrath was withheld from us. This is a heavy truth, but it is essential if we are to grow in our relationships with Christ and avoid the deceptions of false Gospels:

> Pay careful attention to yourselves and to all the flock, in which the Holy Spirit has made you overseers, to care for the church of God, which he obtained with his own blood. I know that after my departure fierce wolves will come in among you, not sparing the flock; and from among your own selves will arise men speaking twisted things, to draw away the disciples after them. (Acts 20:28–30)

> Beloved, do not believe every spirit, but test the spirits to see whether they are from God, for many false

prophets have gone out into the world. By this you know the Spirit of God: every spirit that confesses that Jesus Christ has come in the flesh is from God, and every spirit that does not confess Jesus is not from God. This is the spirit of the antichrist, which you heard was coming and now is in the world already. (1 John 4:1–3)

One of the many reasons early Christians developed creeds that clearly stated their beliefs is because they were combating false gospels—even within the first hundred years after Christ's death. It's not a problem that will go away, and we must learn to recognize these distortions of truth. In some instances, they are quite subtle. It is like what was said in the verse from Acts: that even some from within the body of believers will speak twisted things and draw others away from the Word of God and truth of the Gospel of Christ.

What is a simple way any believer, even one new to the faith, can identify questionable teachings? I believe it is by having an understanding of the essential truths of the Gospel message and testing those truths against what others may falsely claim. Later, in the chapter on division, I have laid out the primary essential beliefs we adhere to as Christians.

We'll speak a bit more about it when addressing false views of Christ, but I submit a very simple place to start as a foundational truth of Christianity is Christ as the only means by which we can be saved from our sinful states. By acknowledging this exclusivity, which is unique to world belief systems, we form a foundation by which we can measure other teachings. For example, if someone teaches that Christ is not the only way to be saved, we can easily discern this as a false teaching:

Jesus said to him, "I am the way, and the truth, and the life. No one comes to the Father except through me." (John 14:6)

And there is salvation in no one else, for there is no
other name under heaven given among men by which
we must be saved. (Acts 4:12)

Both of these verses clearly lay out doctrinal truths that Jesus
is the only way to the Father. To call ourselves Christians, we must
accept this truth. Otherwise, we are simply creating a false gospel
ourselves. For most who claim Christianity, that isn't anything new
to hear. The danger of deception for a believer is usually more subtle.

Let's look at three false gospels and the types of damage they
have the potential to cause. From creating doubt about our faith
to causing division among our brothers and sisters in Christ, false
gospels are a serious matter to consider. To address how we guard
ourselves against these, we can look at a few examples of what would
fall into this category.

Prosperity Gospel

The first false gospel to consider does not seem all that bad
on the surface. And in some sense, believing God for favor in life
is not inherently bad. Where this becomes a false view is when it
overtakes all other views of Christ—or when seekers of God are
lured into a false sense of a life of prosperity without difficulty.
Often, for believers deceived by this gospel, their faith is shallow and
easily rocked by troubles in life. If, as this gospel would claim, we
believe God's primary purpose is to shower riches upon us, it will
be contradicting when we suddenly face something other than that
expectation—and it will be much easier to fall away from a faith that
at times comes with a cost.

Gospel of Inclusion/Universalism

Another distortion of the Gospel is that everyone will eventually
receive a "get out of hell" free card. The Universalist view is related

to our very human view that God is solely love and that a loving God would not send people to a place of torment. This view fails to account for God's nature of justice and holiness in favor of a fluffier, politically correct version of God. This also assumes our emotional, feeling-based love is the same type of love as God.

While God does lovingly care for us, love is more about action. God's ultimate act of love was in reaching out to lost creation and offering a means of coming back to fellowship with Him. Rejecting this does not make God any less loving. And much like a marriage has understandings in the covenant with one another, so too does God's love come with some requirements. He loves all in a general sense as His creation. Yet, it is a deeper love He has for those in Christ who are restored to fellowship with Him. For those who deny this option or ignore it, God's general blessings eventually do come to an end. Though the rain may fall on the just and unjust, it is only those in Christ who are ultimately in a loving relationship with God (Matthew 5:45).

The problem with a view of hell in which everyone is eventually released is that it negates Christ's suffering for us on the cross. Since Christ died the substitutionary death on the cross to keep those who believe in Him out of God's wrath, what was the point if everyone will eventually be saved from it anyway? God offered us a way back into a relationship with Him and made it clear what needed to happen. For some to ignore this and still expect a relationship with God and exception from His justice is foolish. Without the cross and its significance, Christianity becomes just another religion of philosophy and good thoughts. If all sins are eventually overlooked after a time of penance (purgatory) or passing time (universalism)[6] what was the point of suffering on the cross?

As sinful creatures, God is not indebted to us. He owes us nothing. His sacrifice for us with Christ on the cross was done out

---

[6] Zavada, Jack. "What Is Universalism? Learn why universalism is popular, but fatally flawed." Learn Religions, June 25, 2019, https://www.learnreligions.com/what-is-universalism-700701.

of pure mercy. There was nothing we could have done for ourselves, and there still is nothing.

The Universalist view is considered heretical because it denies the very foundation of the Christian faith. Sure, it makes us feel better. It allows our morality to be put in place of God's. We become the judges who decide which sins deserve eternal torment and which sins are bad but not damning. While the world points to Christians as intolerant and arrogant, a worldview in which we place ourselves higher than God is the ultimate in human arrogance.

Believers in Christ will have their works tested for certain, but we are not judged on our eternal destination. Some will say that Christians need not argue about the nature of hell because they won't be going there anyway, but the nature of hell speaks to the nature of our wonderful Creator. Without the conviction of the Holy Spirit, that statement will appear foolish to some. However, it proves that God was so loving that He chose—instead of auto-condemning us—to enter into human history and save those of us who would listen.

While I find the doctrine of universal salvation from hell incompatible with the Bible, I do understand that Christians, secure in their salvation, need not split over this. It is not a salvation issue to someone who already believes in Christ. To those new to the faith, however, it can be detrimental to their growth and sanctification. Paul says we should not create stumbling blocks for our Christian brothers and sisters. The belief in universal salvation from hell also negates accountability. If we are ultimately going to be saved from eternal torment, why not just behave however we choose? We can still love "Jesus the hippie" and His mind-set but ignore the harder aspects of Christianity to live how we want.

This is the implication of an outlook of universalism. We can refrain from using words like heretical if it makes people feel better, but the ultimate truth to this is that it negates the entire foundation of the Christian faith—Christ and His atonement on behalf of us for the remission of the sin that separated us from a holy, just, and loving God. It makes us Buddhists and Hindus in an endless cycle of pointless existence that leads to a mysterious beyond from which we will ultimately be rescued. Christianity is exclusive because Christ said it was exclusive. We understand that apart from Christ, we will be condemned, but for those in Christ, there is no condemnation:

> There is therefore now no condemnation for those who are in Christ Jesus. For the law of the Spirit of life has set you free in Christ Jesus from the law of sin and death. (Romans 8:1–2)

Though salvation in Christ is not meant to just be a ticket to heaven, I would think if people are so worried about making it to heaven, they would accept the requirements to do so. If I give you directions to my house and say it is the only road that will lead there, you wouldn't go driving through fields and forests, thinking you could create a path of your own.

Everyone will hear the Gospel in one form or another. The epistle to the Romans tells us that nature testifies to God—and those who seek Him will find Him. There are even examples of God intervening supernaturally to bring people to Him.

As Christians, we need to acknowledge that there is no doctrine of salvation without a doctrine of hell. What would we be saved from? God's wrath dictates our need for salvation, and in His love, He sent Christ to atone for us and to bear that wrath for us. It's a simple act of belief that has eternally significant implications.

Patriotic Gospel

Popular with conservative Western Christians is the association of God and politics, believing that Jesus cares about our gun rights or other conservative issues that are not biblically relevant. While issues that have a moral component like abortion are certainly issues on which it is worth taking a stand, when we attach our faith completely to our political beliefs, it lessens the impact of the faith. Our political views can be influenced by our faith, but our faith should not be influenced by our political views.

Paul tells us in Romans to be subject to governing authorities for they are placed by God to wield the sword of justice. But much like He used pagan rulers or others who were against Him in the past to achieve His purposes, we cannot assume that every political figure or president who speaks about being for the same things as Christians is necessarily a Christian. Sure, they may be, but we cannot ignore the simple requirements of other believers when it comes to leaders. They are subject to the same law of God and the same requirements of faith.

Some Christians tend to refer to leaders who align with their views as godly or Christian without exploring what it means. God may simply be using nonbelieving leaders to achieve His ultimate purpose—or, in some instances, as discipline to nations that have turned from Him. The patriotic gospel assumes that the United States of America is God's chosen nation and that we can do as we like and still be in His grace as a nation. We begin to feel that God is for us—and every other nation does not know Him or doesn't have the same favor. This creates reasons to treat others as less than us or as not worthy of the same grace of God.

The most heinous evidence of this I've found in my life is when Bible-believing Christians go to a less developed country for mission trips to help the people. They love them and grow from these experiences. Then, when arriving back in the USA, they suddenly become politically active against measures to help those same people. They begin to treat them as inferior and not worthy of the same standard of living we have here. How do we go from caring and loving our neighbors to supporting leaders who want to banish or block our neighbors from opportunities to better themselves?

This is the ultimate danger of the patriotic gospel. An "America first" attitude tied to the Bible and God becomes a dangerous tool for suppressing those we would deem unworthy and leads to pride as a nation that could just as easily be cursed as blessed by God.

False Views of Christ

Moral Teacher Christ

I mentioned this in passing when talking about the false gospel of Universalism, but I will speak to it again here. This view of Christ as simply a moral teacher, human only, and certainly not God incarnate seems to be some sort of middle ground people developed to use for agreeing to disagree about Jesus. For many nonbelievers or those who reject Christ's divinity, this is the preferred view. They boil Jesus down to a moral concept or a teacher of wisdom—and not the Son of God. This eliminates any accountability they would have to a Creator God and allows them to go about their daily lives, unconcerned about Him.

Buddy Christ

There is also the false view of Christ that I call the "Buddy Christ" view. This is the false view of Jesus as one who would never condemn anyone to hell or confront them about their sins. "Hippie Jesus" is another way I've referred to this view. It's the Jesus who's just our good buddy and not part of the Triune God. This is a denial of Christ's own words when He called Himself God and said He was the only way to the Father. It seems like a waste of breath if it weren't true—or at the very least would paint Him as a liar.

If there were many paths to God, then Christ was lying—or misinformed—and therefore not credible. Paul addressed this in his letter to the Corinthians in a bit more detail. If Christ was not who He said He was, and therefore was not raised from the dead, then what is the point of our faith? This was his basic premise in the following verses:

For if the dead are not raised, not even Christ has been raised. And if Christ has not been raised, your faith is futile and you are still in your sins. Then those also who have fallen asleep in Christ have perished. If in Christ we have hope in this life only, we are of all people most to be pitied. (1 Corinthians 15:16–19)

What do I gain if, humanly speaking, I fought with beasts at Ephesus? If the dead are not raised, "Let us eat and drink, for tomorrow we die." (1 Corinthians 15:32)

He implies that there is no meaning to this life without the cross and Christ's resurrection. We might as well follow the hedonistic lifestyle of pleasure in the present and not worry about tomorrow. As great as that will sound to some people, it just puts us further away from God and gives us even less of an excuse on the day when we stand before Him in holy judgment. While it is true for believers that we have a friend in Jesus, we also must realize that were it not for our belief and trust in His sacrifice for our sins, He would most definitely not be categorized as a "friend."

Enlightened Guru

I refer to yoga and its spiritual warfare implications a bit in "The Danger of the Devil." Deepak Chopra's beliefs on topics of spirituality would be a good example of why it is so important to test what is and isn't from God. Though he often makes mention of Christ, it is not Jesus as we would know Him as believers:

"Not the savior, not the one and only Son of God. Rather Jesus embodied the highest level of enlightenment. He spent his brief adult life describing it, teaching it, and passing it on to future generations," he said.[7]

---

[7] Chopra, Deepak. The Third Jesus. (New York: Harmony Publishing, 2009).

Jesus intended to save the world by showing others the path to God-consciousness.[8]

This is a good example of why Eastern philosophies and New Age thought are wholly incompatible with a Christian worldview— and the basis of another false view of Christ as the "enlightened guru." Some Christians have even gotten off track lately by allowing Eastern meditation and yoga practices into the faith, and truthfully, it can be a slippery slope.

Similar to the moral teacher view above, He becomes in line with human men like Mohammed, Confucius, or Buddha—but certainly not unique or divine. This idea of enlightenment and God consciousness has decidedly Eastern roots and calls to mind practices more like Buddhism or even some Hindu deity worship, both of which are incompatible with Christian belief. Yet, like most false belief systems, there are seductive elements to them. The idea that we could achieve enlightenment based solely upon our efforts is certainly appealing to our sinful natures. Humanity longs to embrace full reliance on the self and to observe its truths instead of standing for an absolute standard of truth as the Bible and Christianity do.

The karmic system of good and bad things happening based on good and bad actions is another deceptive concept. And for those who wish to achieve some sort of balance of good versus evil deeds to justify them after death, this system can seem appealing. Do good things, and good things will happen; do bad things, and bad things will happen. It has become a throwaway word in our culture where every celebrity who contributes to a cause is doing it because it's "good karma." Christians do not rely on a system of good versus bad deeds; instead, they cling to the cross of Christ. Why do we do what others do not do? Because Christ's teaching about the nature of God, morality, and truth shows a much different worldview than that proposed by man-made religious systems.

---

[8] Nichols, Michelle. "Who is Jesus? He's three people, says Deepak Chopra." Reuters, February 22, 2008. https://www.reuters.com/article/us-religion-chopra/who-is-jesus-hes-three-people-says-deepak-chopra-idUSN1918295720080221.

It is true that within Buddhism and Hinduism—and many other religions—there is not an exact element of "salvation" as there is with Christianity. This is likely because these religions are totally reliant upon the individual to achieve something. Whether enlightenment, nirvana, good karma, etc., something is being sought after by the individual and by their actions.

Again, the idea of doing good things is not inherently bad. The problem is within these religions and their potential to deceive that they are simply that—religions. Religion will say, "Do this or do that," but Christ says, "It's done." Within the context of Christianity, there is an exclusive claim made by Christ that sets it apart from other faith systems of the world. Christ says humans are not inherently "good." Just as the Bible mentioned plenty of times before Christ, humans have a disease: sin. From the first act against our Creator in the garden, to even the most basic failure we may have today, humanity has issues. Christ tells us that in and of ourselves, we cannot bring about a cure.

These other religious systems will say, "If you balance the amount of good and bad, you can achieve some state of happiness or comfort within the world." Islam has a similar concept in that if you adhere to its tenets (the Five Pillars of Islam), you can achieve favor with the one God (Allah).

Even Judaism, in its current form, relies on some form of good works to earn favor with God. God allowed for a time in ancient Judaism a system of sacrifices and laws meant to temporarily cover the sin (disease) of the people. Like all others since Adam, the Jewish people were dealing with the same "sin problem."

God laid out laws for them as a precursor to what Christ would ultimately achieve on the cross. The sacrificial system of "doing" was a means of showing that, no matter how much they "did," they could never be fully reconciled to God.

And so, viewing Christ as some sort of spiritual guru whose goal was to show us enlightenment or principles that are pulled from these religious systems is viewing a false Christ. While most believers will be aware of this and steer clear, those new in the faith can still be persuaded by some of these Eastern views of Christ and attempts to make Him compatible with these concepts.

Overcoming the Danger of Deception

The danger of deception for Christians mature in their faith may not be as worrisome as for those new to the faith. The best tool and defense for overcoming this danger is knowing the essentials of the faith and standing firm in the Word of God. We will cover those essentials in more detail during an upcoming chapter. Prayer for discernment can go a long way, and some Christians may even have a special gift for this type of discernment. We must not be deceived. Many may claim false views of Christ and His words. Stand firm in the essentials of the faith.

The Danger of the Devil

WHEN DEALING WITH THE DANGERS OF THE CHRISTIAN FAITH, perhaps none is more potentially devastating to Christians than that of our ongoing spiritual battle with the forces of Satan. It is important to note that not everything bad that happens to us is a product of satanic influence (see "The Danger of Doubt" for some other possibilities.) However, we are also not to ignore the clear spiritual battle going on in our midst. A balanced mind-set toward matters of spiritual warfare is the best option.

When we discuss the various other dangers, such as backsliding or compromise in the church, it is easy to see that many of those dangers are brought about primarily because we have the devil as our enemy. To begin, I'll present some background of the entity known as Satan, some of his capabilities, and ultimately how he can negatively affect growing Christians. It is important to note early on that Satan is a creation of God, and therefore fully in His control. He may often be granted a long leash, as is the case in the book of Job, but he is ultimately no more powerful than God allows.

Origins of Satan

Beginning in the book of Genesis, we are introduced to Satan in the form of the serpent who tempts Adam and Eve into disobeying God's direct order. His cunning causes them to question what God had said, and this deception leads them to make that great mistake that can be seen throughout redemptive history. This one act is what all of Christianity ties back to. And though in God's sovereignty, there was always a plan for dealing with it, the effects of sin on the world are a direct product of this initial disobedience, and the subsequent curse put on Adam, Eve, and their descendants by God.

> The serpent said to the woman, "You surely will not die! For God knows that in the day you eat from it your eyes will be opened, and you will be like God, knowing good and evil." (Genesis 3:4–5 NASB)

The temptation of having knowledge more equivalent to that of God is a temptation humankind has faced since that fateful fall from grace. The devil's primary aim in this first deception was causing perfect humankind to fall into sin. Because God's nature cannot tolerate the presence of sin, the fellowship between God and humanity that had previously existed would be broken, and Satan would have some measure of revenge for his initial casting out from heaven after his fall.

God places a curse on humankind and the earth as punishment for the fall. Spiritual and physical death were implemented where before fellowship directly with God and immortality were our privilege. Chapter 3 of the book of Genesis is also where we find the protoevangelium. This is the first biblical prophecy referring to the future redeemer (Christ) who will crush the head of the enemy (Satan), though whose heel must be bruised (death on the cross) for it to be accomplished.

> I will put enmity between you and the woman, and between your offspring and her offspring; he shall bruise your head, and you shall bruise his heel. (Genesis 3:15)

Paul reiterates this point in the book of Romans:

The God of peace will soon crush Satan under your feet. The grace of our Lord Jesus Christ be with you. (Romans 16:20)

In this context, Paul is speaking of the God of peace as Jesus Christ who, by His resurrection and redemptive sacrifice on the cross, has ultimately crushed any hope Satan may have had of a final victory.

Theologically speaking, there are two primary verses Bible scholars will point to, which may refer to the fall of Satan. Let's take a look at the verses that speak primarily of a battle that took place at some time in the history of the universe, in which the archangel Lucifer attempted to overthrow the throne of God:

How you are fallen from heaven, O Day Star, son of Dawn! How you are cut down to the ground, you who laid the nations low! You said in your heart, "I will ascend to heaven; above the stars of God I will set my throne on high; I will sit on the mount of assembly in the far reaches of the north; I will ascend above the heights of the clouds; I will make myself like the Most High." But you are brought down to Sheol, to the far reaches of the pit. (Isaiah 14:12–15)

Isaiah, while prophesying about a known earthly king, enters into phrasing that can only be applied to something beyond earthly context. This happens again as Ezekiel prophesies about another earthly king during his time as a prophet of God:

You were an anointed guardian cherub. I placed you; you were on the holy mountain of God; in the midst of the stones of fire you walked. You were blameless in your ways from the day you were created, till unrighteousness was found in you. In the abundance of your trade you were filled with violence in your midst, and you sinned; so I cast you as a profane thing from the mountain of God, and I destroyed you, O guardian cherub, from the midst of the stones of fire. Your heart was proud because of your beauty; you corrupted your wisdom for the sake of your splendor. I cast you to the ground; I exposed you before kings, to feast their eyes on you. (Ezekiel 28:14–17)

From Ezekiel's description, we gather a bit more information related to Lucifer's fall from heaven. An angel of God of the highest order, Lucifer's beauty and pride caused sin to be found in him, and subsequently, his attempt to overthrow the throne of God sealed his fate. Note the word created used by Ezekiel. This emphasizes one of the most important things to bear in mind when speaking of the danger of the devil. His power and reach are directly sanctioned by God, and his "leash" is only allowed to go as far as God wills it.

The modern cultural depictions of a battle between good and evil in which evil nearly triumphs is an incorrect theological view. Christ is never in danger of being beaten by Satan. It was prophesied that Satan will ultimately be defeated. Even Satan knows this and uses what time he has left to simply take as many people with him in his punishment as possible.

Be sober-minded; be watchful. Your adversary the devil prowls around like a roaring lion, seeking someone to devour. Resist him, firm in your faith, knowing that the same kinds of suffering are being experienced by your brotherhood throughout the world. (1 Peter 5:8–9)

Then I saw an angel coming down from heaven, holding in his hand the key to the bottomless pit and a great chain. And he seized the dragon, that ancient serpent, who is the devil and Satan, and bound him for a thousand years, and threw him into the pit, and shut it and sealed it over him, so that he might not deceive the nations any longer, until the thousand years were ended. After that he must be released for a little while. (Revelation 20:1–3)

Satan is ultimately defeated, bound, released for a time, and then cast out permanently into the lake of fire, which we read was prepared specifically for the devil and his fallen angels. When we refer to demons, we are discussing those angels (one-third of the heavenly host) who rebelled with Satan and were cast out of heaven along with him.

And another sign appeared in heaven: behold, a great red dragon, with seven heads and ten horns, and on his heads seven diadems. His tail swept down a third of the stars of heaven and cast them to the earth. And the dragon stood before the woman who was about to give birth, so that when she bore her child he might devour it … And the great dragon was thrown down, that ancient serpent, who is called the devil and Satan, the deceiver of the whole world—he was thrown down to the earth, and his angels were thrown down with him. (Revelation 12:3–4, 9)

Spiritual Warfare

Satan was the original tempter who caused our first mother and father to fall from God's grace. At the cross, Christ defeated him once and for all, but he is still the god of this earth until Christ returns to set up His kingdom in glory. Because Satan is still active, Christians will still run into the danger of the devil. Often, the closer we draw to God, the more likely we are to experience attacks and temptations from the demonic side of the spiritual realm.

There are several ways in which Satan can influence believers.

Some are actively brought upon us by our actions. Other times, we may passively allow the demonic influences into our lives without realizing it. Still, others are brought about as a means of strengthening our faith in God to overcome the enemy (as was the case with Job).

For the rest of this section, let's analyze the active, passive, and providential means by which Satan and demons can affect the believer in Christ. Bear in mind that Satan cannot possess a believer in Christ for we are already Christ's possessions. The proper terminology concerning believers is that we can potentially be "demonized." Satan's influence can directly affect us, but Satan can never fully possess the true Christian person. Because we are told to always test our salvation and work it out (Philippians 2:12), it is necessary regarding the danger of the devil to be certain we are saved through Christ—so that we will not be overcome by the enemy. Though we may be affected at times, we will always overcome through the blood of Christ and in the name of Jesus when we truly belong to Him.

Active Attacks

Let's first look at ways that Christians actively invite attacks from the enemy. These most often take the form of the temptation toward things we know we ought not to do. New believers, who have just been released from the burden of their sin, are most susceptible to these attacks, though mature believers can also bring about demonic influence in their lives through behaviors that are antithetical to God's command.

For example, a mature Christian believer who actively decides to engage in a sinful activity is potentially inviting demonic spiritual forces to influence his or her life. Backsliding or reverting to sinful ways after our justification in Christ can cause this type of spiritual warfare. When believers try to use grace as a license to sin, they invite attacks from the enemy on their lives. This invitation to Satan by our own active or purposeful failing is a means by which Satan can actively influence believers.

What are some of the results of this influence? For one, we may lose provision or purpose for which God had set us apart. Someone with a measure of leadership in a church, for example, who actively engages in known sin damages their standing of leadership and their witness in the process. Satan loves to latch on to these controversies and attempt to pull believers away from the body as a whole. Through biblical church discipline, fallen believers can often be restored through true repentance and turning from the sin, but for a time, they are often more controlled by evil spiritual forces than good. An example occurs in Paul's first letter to the Corinthian church:

> It is actually reported that there is sexual immorality among you, and of a kind that is not tolerated even among pagans, for a man has his father's wife. And you are arrogant! Ought you not rather to mourn? Let him who has done this be removed from among you. For though absent in body, I am present in spirit; and as if present, I have already pronounced judgment on the one who did such a thing. When you are assembled in the name of the Lord Jesus and my spirit is present, with the power of our Lord Jesus, you are to deliver this man to Satan for the destruction of the flesh, so that his spirit may be saved in the day of the Lord. (1 Corinthians 5:1–5)

In the above verse, the church member in question was involved in a sexual relationship with his stepmother. This was a relationship that he knew was sinful, but in which he continued to engage. Paul is not suggesting the man be killed (destruction of the flesh), but rather through overcoming the flesh (destroying it), the Spirit of God can bring the man about to repentance and turning from his sin. If the man was a true believer, he would desire to turn back to Christ, once disciplined. Paul needs him to be removed from the church body for a time because he does not want that type of behavior to have a negative influence on other believers. This man brought about the active influence of Satan by his choice to be in sin with his stepmother. If his conversion to Christ was true—and this was simply a major stumble in his ultimate sanctification—then Paul's removal of the man from the body of believers should ultimately bring about his repentance and turning from sin. If not, it is likely the man was never really a believer, and he would have already been turned over to Satan. John writes about this similar idea in his first epistle regarding those who appeared to be followers of Christ, but afterward proved they were not. Jesus speaks a bit to this as well in His Sermon on the Mount, emphasizing that not all who have professed faith in Him are actual believers. The following verses can serve as a caution to Christians who would externally appear saved, but inwardly have no actual saving faith:

> They went out from us, but they were not of us; for if they had been of us, they would have continued with us. But they went out, that it might become plain that they all are not of us. (1 John 2:19)

> Not everyone who says to me, "Lord, Lord," will enter the kingdom of heaven, but the one who does the will of my Father who is in heaven. On that day many will say to me, "Lord, Lord, did we not prophesy in your name, and cast out demons in your name, and do many mighty works in your name?" And then will I declare to them, "I never knew you; depart from me, you workers of lawlessness." (Matthew 7:21–23)

Believers who are actively being influenced by Satan are somewhat rarer these days because we have the whole of biblical and church history as an example of what God expects of us. Though we are justified, and ultimately forgiven, for our sins, we are still to follow God's commands, and active rebellion against the commands is more often a sign of unbelief than the stumbling of true believers (though new believers would likely be more susceptible early on to this type of rebellion).

Another example of actively inviting demonic influence on our lives as believers would be visiting fortune-tellers or other such places. These practices are strictly forbidden in scripture, and they most definitely open us up to demonic influence. I will speak more about them in the passive section as well; in many cases, the believer may not be aware of how abominable these practices are to the Lord, and therefore might participate unknowingly. Unfortunately, some still see no harm and engage in these activities while still claiming to walk in the Christian faith.

Passive Attacks

The passive influence of Satan on believers is a much more common problem in modern times than many realize. Christians, to be more appealing to the culture as a whole, often let things into their lives that invite the presence of the demonic, and very often, they don't realize they are doing it. We will explore some examples of this in terms of objects, cultural practices, and incompatible beliefs merged with Christianity.

Objects

The influence on a believer by objects of a demonic nature is probably the most overlooked of the possible means of passively experiencing demonic influence in our walks. Pastor Matt White of Calvary Worship Center in Austin tells the story of a gift that was given to him, which ultimately ended up creating a demonic influence upon his whole house. He had hung the item upon a corkboard in the house and thought nothing of it. However, for multiple nights, he awoke suddenly to a clear demonic influence upon the room. On a hunch, he began doing some research on the gift and discovered it was a Native American dream catcher. These dream catchers are items of demonic influence in that they are often blessed in ceremonies by shaman and dedicated to worship of demonic deities.

Once Matt got rid of the dream catcher, the demonic influence over his house was removed—and all returned to normal. Many items like this seem harmless on the surface. We probably played with them as kids. I used to have a lucky rabbit's foot, and I know for sure my brother used to have a dream catcher over his bed. As children, we had no idea of the influence of these items, and perhaps since we were not yet believers, the influence was minimal. However, there is evidence that items of this nature have demonic connotation whether or not we acknowledge it. For believers, this can create danger with the devil. Even something like a Magic 8-Ball can be considered an object of divination and contain with it the influence of Satan (though perhaps on a much lesser level).

It is worth noting that not all believers are attacked in the same way in spiritual warfare. Satan will often target us in areas of weakness. If a believer is not tempted by alcohol, likely Satan wouldn't use alcohol as a means of temptation. However, if that same believer had struggled with pornography in the past, Satan might use that in some way to affect the believer's life and exert demonic spiritual influence over them. Though these influences cannot cancel out true salvation in Christ, they can cause troubles in our lives or impact the spiritual growth for which God has us in mind.

Another object or symbol that is commonly found with believers is the peace sign. This sign appears harmless on the surface but is representative of a broken cross and is sometimes used in witchcraft. We should not have these types of items in the house or wear clothing promoting these items if we wish to purge ourselves of potential demonic influence.

In What the Bible Says About Spiritually Cleansing Your Home, Betty Miller writes,

> We should also check our homes to see what kind of
> pictures we have on the walls and check our closets
> for old souvenirs of the past and ask the Holy Spirit

to show us the things of darkness that should not be in our homes. It would be wise to throw out the old weather witches (don't become involved with "water witching" either), Ouija boards, wooden spoons with evil faces from foreign islands, excessive owl and frog decorator items, sun-gods, Confucius paintings, images of serpents and dragons, voodoo dolls, Kachina dolls, Yeibichai designs on Indian rugs, Indian "god's-eye" objects made with yarn, dream catchers, etc.[9]

There are several other items of this nature, and the full article by Miller has them listed. Though this could be construed as a personal preference situation with believers, one could also argue, as Miller does, that it's more of an essential. Verses like Deuteronomy 7:25 say we should burn the graven images of other gods. Very often, these seemingly harmless household objects have some relation to the worship of a false god or demonic entity. Referring to articles of clothing a believer may choose to wear with one of these symbols or objects, Betty writes:

> People who wear anti-Christian symbols open themselves up to the works of darkness such as depression, lust, moodiness, sickness, accidents, fear, etc.[10]

Though it may seem extreme to rid your house of these objects and symbols, the ultimate spiritual benefit is worth the effort. Our sanctification—the ongoing attempt to live more like Christ from day to day—is difficult enough without adding these satanic influences into our lives, even if by accident.

---

[9] Miller, Betty with Janice Fritch. "What the Bible Says about Spiritually Cleansing Your Home." Bible Resources. org. March 12, 2014, https://bibleresources.org/spiritually-cleansing-home/.
[10] Ibid.

Cultural Practices

Cultural practices that can result in passive demonic influence include, most often, participation in festivals or holidays that have demonic undertones. The most common one to explore would be that of Halloween. Overall, I've come to the conclusion that participation in Halloween ultimately comes down to a personal preference for believers. Though, it cannot be denied there are some demonic undertones to the day as a whole.

For believers who have previously struggled with the occult, it would be wise to steer clear of these types of holiday practices. Like Halloween in the United States, the Day of the Dead in Mexico—with its emphasis on death and skulls—is another holiday that opens up realms of the demonic. Praying for dead ancestors is more associated with pagan practices than anything in the realm of Christianity.

Another activity commonly done by modern Christians is that of yoga. There is quite a lot of debate among Christians as to whether or not this is harmless, but what cannot be argued is its origins in Hindu deity worship. The yoga positions are each associated with a specific prayer or movement of respect to Hindu gods—and therefore are quite demonic in their action. For those who do not see the potential demonic influence, we can only ask that the Holy Spirit open our eyes to anything in our lives that may be causing passive demonic influence. Believers should also not be involved in the reading of horoscopes or studying the birth signs. This falls into the realm of astrology, which is also forbidden in scripture:

> When you come into the land that the Lord your God is giving you, you shall not learn to follow the abominable practices of those nations. There shall not be found among you anyone who burns his son or his daughter as an offering, anyone who practices divination or tells fortunes or interprets omens, or a sorcerer or a charmer or a medium or a necromancer or one who inquires of the dead, for whoever does

these things is an abomination to the Lord. And because of these abominations the Lord your God is driving them out before you. (Deuteronomy 18:9–14)

Though not exhaustive, this list of forbidden practices in Deuteronomy is typically considered all-encompassing for anything that seeks to undermine faith and trust in God in favor of inquiry by humanity into the spirit realm. Consulting of mediums, fortune-tellers, and the use of tarot cards are all completely forbidden to Christians. Those who still participate in these rituals are actively sinning and opening themselves up to demonic influence and oppression.

Incompatible Belief

In terms of the passive attack of believers by Satan, we must also consider the mixing of beliefs that are incompatible with Christianity. Like objects and cultural practices above, there is some overlap in our discussion. For incompatible belief, the primary example I will use is that of the integration of Eastern religion with Christianity.

Many Christians still have statues of Buddha or posters of various Hindu deities in their homes. In most cases, if they are truly believers, it is unintentional, and the items just seem like cool decorations. Like the objects mentioned above, statues of Buddha or Hindu gods and goddesses are a surefire way to bring the influence of the demonic upon believers or their households. Eastern religions and New Age philosophies are inherently anti-Christian. Worship of multiple deities, adherence to self, and other elements of these religions are directly incompatible with the teachings of Christ. Satan often will attack the believer spiritually through these items and false beliefs.

Frequently, these passive attacks from the spiritual realm are due to a believer's lack of knowledge. It is wise, then, to inquire of the Holy Spirit that He would reveal to us any items or practices in which we are engaged that are actively bringing demonic influence into our lives.

Providential Attack

The most difficult types of attack from Satan for humans to understand are those that are allowed by God as a means of testing. The Bible gives us some great examples of believers who were tested by God through Satan and ultimately triumphed and came out stronger on the other end. It is important to clarify that it is Satan initiating these attacks—or a product of sin in the world as a whole—but God can use these existing circumstances for His purpose in the believer's life. The primary example which comes to mind is that of Job. The book of Job begins with this statement:

> There was a man in the land of Uz whose name was Job, and that man was blameless and upright, one who feared God and turned away from evil. (Job 1:1)

From the very beginning, we learn that Job is right with God and not engaged in any active or passive rebellion. However, he experiences an attack from Satan to a degree not often seen in the life of a believer. This attack is allowed by God to prove to Satan that Job will remain true to Him, regardless of circumstances.

God gives Satan restrictions on what he can and cannot do to Job, once again indicating that God has sovereign control over all that Satan is allowed to do and that Satan cannot act without God's expressed permission.

I encourage readers to read the entire book of Job for a more in-depth study. What we learn within its pages is that Job did nothing specifically wrong to cause Satan to attack him. Theologically, the book of Job helps prove that our pain and suffering are not always a result of anything we've done. They are often meant as a time of testing and trial to grow us in our reliance on God. They are often meant to show that—even in our affliction—He is still present and active in our lives as believers. We may not always understand during the trouble, but on the other side, we can see God present with us throughout the suffering. He will carry us through to the other side. We need only trust Him fully in good times and bad.

Jesus was also tempted by Satan in the wilderness—not because of anything He actively did but because that temptation was sanctioned as a means of allowing Jesus to resist without sinning. Jesus leaned on the Word of God to combat Satan, and that is always the believers' best tool in the spiritual battle.

Overcoming the Danger of the Devil

The Word of God and the name of Jesus are our protection against demonic forces. As Paul says, we are waging an ongoing war against principalities and powers of the air and not flesh and blood:

> For we do not wrestle against flesh and blood, but against the rulers, against the authorities, against the cosmic powers over this present darkness, against the spiritual forces of evil in the heavenly places. (Ephesians 6:12)

The danger of the devil is always present in the lives of believers, and we must be ready to face this spiritual battle. The closer we draw to God, the more we will be susceptible to spiritual attacks. Satan knows his time is limited, and as Peter mentioned, he is seeking whomever he can devour in the time he has left.

Understanding how we actively, passively, and providentially are open to these demonic forces will help us better prepare ourselves for battle. We must equip ourselves daily with the armor of God—and always be vigilant about the ways in which Satan tries to influence us. Only then can we resist the wiles of the enemy and grow in our walks with Christ and the fulfillment of our purpose for the Lord in this life.

Therefore, take up the whole armor of God, that you may be able to withstand in the evil day, and having done all, to stand firm. Stand therefore, having fastened on the belt of truth, and having put on the breastplate of righteousness, and, as shoes for your feet, having put on the readiness given by the Gospel of peace. In all circumstances take up the shield of faith, with which you can extinguish all the flaming darts of the evil one; and take the helmet of salvation, and the sword of the Spirit, which is the word of God, praying at all times in the Spirit, with all prayer and supplication. To that end, keep alert with all perseverance, making supplication for all the saints, and also for me, that words may be given to me in opening my mouth boldly to proclaim the mystery of the Gospel. (Ephesians 6:13–19)

The Danger of Division

I READ AN INTERESTING STORY THAT WAS CIRCULATING ONLINE A FEW months ago. It is likely fictional, but it serves to illustrate an important point regarding the danger of division for Christians.

A lady went to her pastor and said, "Pastor, I won't be going to your church anymore."

The pastor responded, "But why?"

The lady said, "Ah! I saw a woman gossiping about another member; a man who is a hypocrite; the worship team living wrong; people looking at their phones during service; among so many other things wrong in your church."

The pastor replied "Okay. But before you go, do me a favor: take a full glass of water and walk around the church three times without spilling a drop on the ground. Afterward, leave the church if you desire."

The lady thought, Too easy! She walked three times around the church as the pastor had asked. When she finished, she told the pastor she was ready to leave.

The pastor said, "Before you leave, I want to ask you one more question. When you were walking around the church, did you see anyone gossiping?"

The lady replied, "No."

"Did you see any hypocrites?"

The lady said, "No."

"Anyone looking at their phone?"

"No."

"You know why?"

"No."

"You were focused on the glass to make sure you didn't stumble and spill any water. It's the same with our life. When we keep our eyes on Jesus, we don't have time to see the mistakes of others. We will reach out a helping hand to them and concentrate on our own walk with the Lord."[11]

> I appeal to you, brothers, by the name of our Lord Jesus Christ, that all of you agree, and that there be no divisions among you, but that you be united in the same mind and the same judgment. For it has been reported to me by Chloe's people that there is quarreling among you, my brothers. What I mean is that each one of you says, "I follow Paul," or "I follow Apollos" or "I follow Cephas," or "I follow Christ." Is Christ divided? Was Paul crucified for you? Or were you baptized in the name of Paul? (1 Corinthians 1:10–13)

Is Christ divided? Paul brings up an issue that we face even today. There are such a great number of denominations and variations on the original teachings of Christ that it is difficult for even a few groups to agree with one another on everything. The church is the body of Christ. How can that body function if its parts are each doing their own thing?

The danger of division affects Christians directly. It has the potential to cause an implosion from the inside out. It also paints a rather bleak picture of Christ's body as a whole. How could so many who follow the teachings of Christ and profess to have accepted Him into their lives by faith and repentance be in such disagreement? To examine this danger, let us look to a few areas in the Christian walk where it is possible to find sources of disagreement and division in the body.

---

[11] Johnson, Mel. "Pastor Uses Glass of Water to Teach Complaining Woman a Lesson." God Updates, July 28, 2017. https://www.godupdates.com/pastor-glass-of-water-focus-parable/.

Personal Preferences

One problem we face as the church is that the Bible simply does not put every single direction for us in black and white. It is authoritative, yes, but in many of today's primary issues, we don't get a specific sentence telling us whether or not to do something. This leads to disagreements over personal preferences and actual doctrine. For example, should Christians celebrate Halloween? I've heard many views on this, and in all honesty, without bending some verses to our will, we don't get Christ or the Bible specifically saying, "Thou shalt not celebrate Halloween." We do get a strong indication that sorcery, witchcraft, and much of what appears to be celebrated during Halloween are abominations to God, but one might argue it's just an excuse for kids to dress up and get candy. Some Christians might say it's for the kids anyway—and there shouldn't be anything wrong with celebrating this holiday.

Or perhaps the church will try to put on an alternative to Halloween. They'll allow costumes and candy but serve it out of car trunks and tailgates in the parking lot. This attempt to keep kids from the world's version of the celebration (door-to-door trick-or-treating) is one way in which compromise has been attempted. Others may use it as a time to go door-to-door, handing out pamphlets on salvation.

Yet the one thing these all have in common is that they acknowledge and do something on that particular day. Rather than doing this type of seemingly harmless practice for their children on any other day (dressing up, eating candy, etc.), they choose to participate on the same date that the world celebrates, and this is where some might say a potential problem lies.

In my experience, a good majority of Christians in the United States do some sort of costume and candy activity on October 31. However, my wife grew up in Mexico, and Halloween and Day of the Dead, a few days later, were not celebrated by her family. When she first came to the United States, she was adamant that, as Christians, we should completely ignore this holiday and not participate in it. I'm inclined to agree as the years have gone by.

Can I state that a Christian who celebrates Halloween is sinning or directly violating a biblical principle? I don't believe so. It's a matter of personal preference, though, with relevant concerns. My purpose is to speak in more general terms. That is simply one example, but it brings up the issues of personal preference over essential doctrine, which I will discuss further in this section.

Personal preferences for Christians would be practices that are not specifically condemned in the Bible but are also not necessarily promoted. Drinking alcohol is one. Dancing in some Baptist churches is another. Church of Christ denominations frowned upon the use of instruments in worship. These are all more a matter of either church or personal preferences.

Regarding some of these examples, the Bible does not specifically say not to drink alcohol at all, but rather not to be drunk with alcohol. It doesn't say to only sing hymns in service or only contemporary songs. It doesn't specify having a drum set or not. Though worship styles may certainly cause division at times, it seems more relevant to discuss a preference that falls more into a gray area, such as Christians and the drinking of alcohol. While many Christians will choose not to touch alcohol (and I support that decision), some may choose to have a beer or a glass of wine with dinner. The Bible forbids drunkenness—but not specifically having a drink. Though we should clarify that when the Bible speaks of wine, it is referring to a very watered-down version compared to what we would call wine today. Is it all right to have a drink? Biblically, someone could make that case, yes. However, Paul does mention specific situations in which doing so could be detrimental to the faith of those still new to their Christian walk:

> Therefore, as to the eating of food offered to idols, we know that "an idol has no real existence," and that "there is no God but one." (1 Corinthians 8:4)

> But take care that this right of yours does not somehow become a stumbling block to the weak. For if anyone

sees you who have knowledge eating in an idol's temple, will he not be encouraged, if his conscience is weak, to eat food offered to idols? And so by your knowledge this weak person is destroyed, the brother for whom Christ died. Thus, sinning against your brothers and wounding their conscience when it is weak, you sin against Christ. Therefore, if food makes my brother stumble, I will never eat meat, lest I make my brother stumble. (1 Corinthians 8:9–13, see also Romans 14:13–19)

Paul seems to answer the question about preferences and doctrine pretty clearly in this chapter. He is saying in his example that Christians understood if they ate meat that had previously been sacrificed to an idol, that it was simply the practice of the meat sellers of the day. They understood, as mature Christians, that the idol was not real or present in the meat. In some cases, it was ruder to refuse to eat than not to eat. However, Paul goes on to make himself clearer with the caveat to this personal preference. If a younger brother or sister in the faith is present, it is wiser to refuse to eat the sacrificed meat.

To put it in terms of our example, if we can have a beer or glass of wine without drunkenness as a Christian, it would still be wiser not to drink at all in the presence of one not as mature in the faith, lest the wrong impressions be given (Romans 14:13–15; 20–23). In this way, though, many church divisions have arisen, and from them denominational differences on higher levels than simply whether or not a Christian can drink alcohol, dance, or engage in some other preferential practice. Paul does say further on, however, that while some things may be permissible, not all are helpful to a believer's growth:

"All things are lawful," but not all things are helpful. "All things are lawful," but not all things build up.

Let no one seek his own good, but the good of his
neighbor. (1 Corinthians 10:23–24)

In the above verse, Paul is restating a belief the Corinthian church
was following, specifically that "all things are lawful." He used their
existing system of belief against them by directly answering the
quotes from the Corinthians. The Corinthians say, "All things are
lawful," and Paul says, "But not all things are helpful." This would
indicate that Paul believed not all things are lawful—and that many
things are unhelpful to the believer.

A more recent example relevant to this verse is the ongoing
debate about whether or not we should wear masks and maintain
social distancing to slow the spread of the COVID-19 virus. Perhaps
because it has become a politicized topic, more division is arising than
we might have expected. Sadly, much of that division is happening
between Christians.

The last portion of 1 Corinthians 10:23–24 says we should seek
the good of our neighbors above our own. What better way to love
our neighbor than to proactively do something that could help lower
the chance of exposing them to sickness? The danger of COVID-19
seems to be primarily that someone could be a carrier yet show no
symptoms. With that in mind, if we are to be in public places among
others who may be more susceptible to the virus, it is more loving
to our neighbor to wear a mask and keep our distance. It may be
uncomfortable, but we show the love of Christ in protecting others.
Christ tells us to love one another. Can we really say we love our
neighbor and then risk exposing them to a virus that we can't be
certain we do or do not have?

Just because it may be lawful to forego wearing a mask or social
distancing does not mean it is helpful, which we could argue from
Paul's statements. To me, this is particularly applicable in physical
church gatherings. For churches that must meet physically—or choose
to do so during our current pandemic—it is most loving to require at
the very least some distancing, and ideally facial coverings. Leaving
it up to the individual members ultimately means higher risk to the

body as a whole. If we all come together and practice some caution, it provides the most benefit to everyone—even though it will mean a small sacrifice of comfort.

When does a personal preference become a source of actual division? I would suggest that it occurs when one believer's personal preference is imposed upon another believer as though it were an essential doctrine. Though we are right to stand by our convictions, often, if we stand too firmly, we can create hostility or division within the church body. We must distinguish the essentials of the faith over personal preferences and even the doctrinal nonessentials that we tend to get worked up over as believers. An example would be denominational splits regarding something like the way the end of time could come about. While we understand Christ is coming again, many disagree on what this looks like.

As a young, fiery-eyed college student, I remember studying the book of Revelation quite deeply after reading the Left Behind book series. I decided the way I was reading it was absolutely the way things were going to happen. I had the time lines ready, and I could tell you what to expect. I couldn't tell you when it would begin, but I could tell you what my view said would happen after that point.

I remember naively trying to lead a Bible study on the book of Revelation at my home church, which was Methodist and not big on eschatology in the first place, and I was met with quite a bit of disapproval and division over my views. It's not that the views I shared were wrong necessarily, but I was pushing them so hard as the only acceptable view that it was creating division.

While the end-times and Christ's return are essentially important, how it comes about is not essential to our salvation and therefore is not worth dividing over. There are many doctrinal issues of this nature as well. Should there be so much division over minor issues like these? Personally, I think not.

When our personal preferences become so much of a focus that we become hostile to those who don't believe the same as we do, we create division. As imperfect beings, we have many idiosyncrasies that manifest themselves in a variety of less-than-Christlike ways.

It is important to note here that I'm not talking about disagreements about the essentials. Christians, regardless of denominational lines, if they are truly in Christ, will believe in certain essentials of the faith. Let's examine some of these before going further to better prepare ourselves to discern these essentials from personal preferences.

Christian Essential Beliefs

Many have documented and discussed our essential Christian beliefs before me, and many of the church creeds lay them out well. For this section on Christian essential beliefs, I'd like to borrow from a section of a book by Pastor Mike Fabarez. His layout of the essentials leading to salvation helps break it down simply. I am paraphrasing but using his general statements and ideas throughout.

First, as Christians, we believe God is our Creator and the originator of all things. As such, we must give an account to Him. We believe God is holy. He is the standard of good by which all other standards must be measured. Before we came to Christ, we were sinful and separated from God, and in our unholiness, we could not be in fellowship without some sort of mediator. We believe that God also is just and must resolve the wrongs committed against His holy standard. Because of this, we deserved God's punishment. As the Bible says, none are righteous (Psalm 14:3, 53:1–3; Romans 3:10–12).

These first essentials about God form the foundation on which the Gospel (the good news) rests. We must hear this rather disheartening news—and believe it—to fully understand the significance of the Gospel and our salvation in Christ. We believe God is also loving. In His ultimate kindness and desire for the well-being of His creation, He orchestrated a means by which the fellowship with Him could be renewed. The only means of salvation is Jesus Christ (John 14:6; Acts 4:12).

God was the only one capable of solving this sin problem, and so He stepped into time and space to live as a perfect human and fulfill all the holy requirements of human righteousness. He came as both fully God and fully man, laying aside some of His divine attributes willingly—but never losing His divinity (Philippians 2:5–11). In the Old Testament, the sacrifices of spotless animals did not eliminate sin, but they provided an example of the substitution that was needed and our inability to achieve this by anything we could do. Our sin problem needed a substitute.

Christ suffered the judgment for the sin we deserve so that we could be treated by God as though we lived sinless lives.[12]

We believe that Christ's resurrection proved that the power of sin and death was defeated, our fellowship with God repaired, and the future promise of the resurrection of our bodies after death to spend eternity with God was secured. As Christians, we believe in the forgiveness of sin found only in Christ's sacrifice on the cross. Salvation by repentance and faith alone, not by works, and in bearing fruit once saved as an outpouring of good deeds and daily desire to obey God's commands more fully. These foundational beliefs are necessary to call ourselves Christians.

There are other essentials such as the authority and inerrancy of scripture, the virgin birth, and the Triune God (Father, Son, and Holy Spirit). I believe that the final destinations of heaven or hell are also essential to our belief and help clarify why there was a need for Christ's sacrifice. The prospect of our heavenly existence as believers should also inspire joy and anticipation, which I'll speak a bit more to this in a later chapter.

Moving back to our discussion of church divisions, if a church divides over the essentials of Christianity, it is often best to let those in disagreement go their own way. However, if we are losing Christians because they can't agree on how the end-times will occur or because the drums are too loud at church, that's where unnecessary division is occurring.

One particular source of division within the churches I have attended over the years is what I have dubbed the "church mafia."

---

[12] Fabarez, Mike. 10 Mistakes People Make About Heaven, Hell, and the Afterlife, (Eugene, OR: 2018), 185–191.

This is not an actual mafia organization; it is a select group of individuals whose personal worship and seating preferences dictate that of other congregants. For example, the family who has had multiple generations in the particular congregation, who has always sat on the advisory board, and in the same seat week after week will be particularly vulnerable to being part of this church mafia syndrome. People tend to consider themselves important in matters of which all should be equal. Multiple family generations in a congregation should be celebrated, but that should not be a free pass to deny another member a seat or a voice at church meetings. In many mainline denominational churches, we see division developing as the church mafia presents an air of exclusion that causes those new to the congregation to feel uncomfortable. The early church shared all they had with one another, and arguments over seating charts or order of worship were few and far between, I would imagine.

> For if a man wearing a gold ring and fine clothing comes into your assembly, and a poor man in shabby clothing also comes in, and if you pay attention to the one who wears the fine clothing and say, "You sit here in a good place," while you say to the poor man, "You stand over there," or, "Sit down at my feet," have you not then made distinctions among yourselves and become judges with evil thoughts? (James 2:2–4)

Church Hopping Creates Division

In some ways, we now have too much control over the type of worship we experience. This new abundance of options has the potential to cause division and dissatisfaction. It also brings personal preference into an act of worship that should be focused on the object of worship (Christ) regardless of music or worship styles. This abundance of choices is one possible factor in the dangerous divisions that often present themselves among believers. It is because of such an effect that people often leave churches over very petty issues. In a culture where you can have everything as you want it, people are free to pick and choose the church that matches their personality.

For example, the church someone started attending because they had a built-in coffee shop for their morning fix may decide one day to have a more traditional, hymn-based worship service. For a modern, coffee shop-loving Christian, this flashback to a worship style that is less than contemporary could be a reason for them to bail on that congregation in search of their next fix. I like how Pastor Paul Sheppard of Destined for Victory Ministries put it in one of his recorded messages: "The kingdom of God is not Burger King; you can't have it your way!"

Often, a church will see sudden growth simply because another church in the area had some sort of division—and much of that congregation distributed themselves to other churches. That is not the type of growth the church should seek. Chances are if something bothered them enough to leave the first church, the new church will eventually manage to offend and cause them to move on to yet another. This church hopping is very detrimental to the body of Christ.

In The 10 Dumbest Things Christians Do, Mark Atteberry categorizes these "church hoppers." The first category is the complainer:

> The complaining church hopper is never satisfied. He finds fault with everything the church does and foolishly believes the church down the highway will be exactly what he's looking for.

The second category of church hopper is the consumer:

> Church A might have an awesome worship band, while church B has a preacher you love to listen to. But then one of your buddies who attends Church C asks you to play on their softball team … Is this a

problem? Of course not! You just do what any good consumer would do. You hop back and forth between the three churches.[13]

Church hoppers are "like a lover with a wandering eye, always on the hunt for something better," according to Joshua Harris, author of *Stop Dating the Church.*[14]

In the culture of consumerism that makes up much of the United States, we find that everyone can pick and choose what they want and don't want. When applied to a believer trying to find a church home, it becomes nearly impossible to settle down if one is approaching it with this type of consumer attitude. Despite all of this, we should not be of the impression that attending church is optional.

And let us consider how to stir up one another to love and good works, not neglecting to meet together, as is the habit of some, but encouraging one another, and all the more as you see the Day drawing near. (Hebrews 10:24–25)

Is this church-hopping consumerism any better than simply staying home in bed on a Sunday morning? And what are the essential things a believer should be looking for in a church home? We must first narrow it down to churches that preach the Word of God and stand firm on the foundation of the truth of the Gospel.

For a believer, especially one new to the faith, fellowship found within a physical meeting of others is essential to growth. We cannot be solo Christians and grow or mature in Christ, trying to do it without others. And the best place to find others, however flawed they may sometimes be, is in the church. A foolproof way to find satisfaction in a church home is to serve. Service can be something

---

[13] Atteberry, Mark. The 10 Dumbest Things Christians Do, (Nashville: 2006), 84.
[14] Harris, Joshua. "Stop Dating the Church." Outreach Magazine. August 11, 2011. https://churchleaders.com/outreach-missions/outreach-missions- articles/138766-stop-dating-the-church.html articles/138766-stop-dating-the-church.html.

as simple as greeting at the door to taking up the offering. We can use our talents to serve in a variety of ways. Not everyone has to be on stage preaching or a member of the worship team. When we realize we can do our own parts, it makes attending a church a gratifying experience that can challenge and grow us in our faith.

My wife and I struggled after moving to Austin, Texas, from Oklahoma in 2009 because we didn't have a solid church home. We managed to miss out on church for that entire first year. In 2010, one random morning, we walked into the service at a church near where we were living. At that time in our lives, the message spoke to us, the worship pulled us in, and we felt God calling us back to Him (after a dry season of not attending).

We grew in many ways at that church, including finally learning the importance of tithing and what it represented. I was also able to play consistently in the worship band and pursue that area of my gifting. Over time, however, we realized that this church did not offer as much in terms of maturing the believers in their knowledge of biblical truth. They spoke biblical truth, but it was rarely challenging. They had great motivational messages for sure, and for new believers in Christ, it was perfect. However, we began to seek more meat—as Paul would say—instead of staying and only subsisting on milk. On a positive note, a great pastoral relationship developed between the associate pastor and me, and we made many friends while there.

The first church we attended after that one became the standard by which we would measure all others. The teaching and preaching were strong. It had a great focus on missions—my wife's determining criteria—and the small groups offered a chance to grow more outside of just Sunday mornings. We attended this church for the next four years. During this time, I also began leading worship at a church plant that met on Saturday nights. It had been started by the associate pastor I mentioned before from the first church.

Around 2015, this pastor friend was called to take over another congregation for two years. He asked me to be a part-time worship leader, and I accepted. It was the logical next move since I had been part of his small church plant for three years. The drawback was that his church now met on Sunday mornings, and it became impossible to attend our primary home church. As much as I loved leading worship and pursuing what God was calling me to, this period caused some neglect with my wife, who was much happier in our home church. Ultimately, with the birth of our daughter in 2017, we moved back to Oklahoma and are plugged in and serving with our church family here.

I explain all of this background to point out that I do believe various circumstances can justify the swapping of churches. In the previous examples, my wife and I never left for negative reasons. It wasn't because of complaints we had—unless you count not getting enough teaching a challenge. It was growing in our faith and letting God move us where we felt called during various seasons.

This all occurred within about six years, and in the grand scheme of things, we weren't so entrenched in any congregation long enough that it felt like a betrayal to leave. However, we learned that doing things on our own—without a body of believers to support us and keep us accountable—never worked. Christians need to be part of a body of believers who believe and preach the essential truths of the faith. They also need to seek harmony within the body and not dissension.

In his book, Atteberry also mentions six characteristics of the chronic church hopper. Though we switched between a couple of churches, we were not doing it for any of the following reasons. Atteberry says that church hoppers:

- tend to be very critical
- tend to have a "me-first" attitude
- almost never get involved
- almost never make a serious financial investment in the church
- make it a point to remain emotionally detached
- enjoy living free from accountability[15]

---

[15] Atteberry, The 10 Dumbest Things Christians Do, 93.

My wife and I were not overly critical of the first church we left. We also moved much farther north in town at one point, and the drive became another determining factor. Based on Atteberry's criteria, I would say that my wife and I were not the negative types of church hopper that he mentions in his book. I suspect that many who are reading this also would not fall into the negative category—even if they have had two or three church homes over the past ten years.

It is immensely helpful to read the doctrinal statements of a church one is about to attend. Right off the bat, it should give a clear understanding of that church's core beliefs. If too many don't align with our own, it is probably best not to involve ourselves there—even if they have the best coffee. Many believers don't understand what they believe. They claim Christianity in title—but not in actively seeking growth and sanctification in Christ. Peter speaks to both of these things in his epistles:

> Therefore, brothers, be all the more diligent to confirm your calling and election, for if you practice these qualities you will never fall. (2 Peter 1:10)

> In your hearts honor Christ the Lord as holy, always being prepared to make a defense to anyone who asks you for a reason for the hope that is in you; yet do it with gentleness and respect. (1 Peter 3:15)

We are justified at our moment of conversion, but we constantly seek growth and want to become more like Christ. This is what Peter means in making our calling sure. Our salvation, being purchased by Christ, should lead us to want to grow in our love and knowledge of Him. We must plant ourselves within a church body that preaches biblically. This environment can do wonders for our growth as believers in Christ and is something many Christians are lacking. Complacency is another reason people do not grow. They find a church with good coffee, good music, and a decent preacher, and they settle in for the long haul, never realizing there are more edifying church bodies they could be seeking. If someone is not growing, there is reason to leave and look for another congregation.

So, is there justification for moving between churches? I believe it is acceptable in certain circumstances, namely something that is going to mature us as believers or allow us to fulfill a calling God may be putting on our heart. I do not believe it is acceptable to leave due to a petty complaint, such as the music being too loud, the coffee not tasting good, or any other non-biblical, opinion-based reason. Within the danger of division, it is those believers—or those claiming belief—who bounce around churches due to petty reasons that can cause strife within the body. Let us be humble in our spirits and not forceful in our opinions. Let us accept where God places us in His will for the seasons we are placed and not seek to disrupt any church body, whether members or just visitors. In this way, we can effectively avoid the battles that often cause division within the body of Christ.

Political Division

With the current state of political affairs in the US, many Christians have divided themselves more than usual. The Christians on the right believe those on the left are not Christians and vice versa. I've seen families arguing with one another about which political side is more correct, knowing full well they were all Bible-believing Christians.

We cannot let our political differences divide our faith. There are true believers on both sides of the political spectrum. This comes down a bit to what I mentioned previously about essentials and nonessentials. The candidate we vote for as president does have an effect on the world as a whole, but in regard to Christianity, it is nonessential.

Biblically, we are told numerous times to respect those in authority—and to only resist if a law goes fully against God's Word or puts a Christian in a position where they must either compromise between God or the legality of an issue (Romans 13). However, far from experiencing this type of persecution in the United States, Christians are just disagreeing on issues that mean something to them personally, and they are fighting one another when two viewpoints don't align.

Regarding our mask discussion, a government mandate to wear masks in the interest of protecting others is not persecution, and obeying the mandates in this type of circumstance is the more biblical practice. Even limiting the number of people who could safely gather earlier this year, which caused some churches to only hold online services for a while, was not persecution of Christians. It was simply a measure to protect everyone—Christian or not.

Part of being a unique individual is our ability to believe what we want. We should be less focused on condemning our brothers and sisters in Christ over their personal political views, and more focused on spreading the Gospel of Christ to a world that is very much in need.

Whether the president is a Democrat or Republican has no immediate bearing on our ability to share the good news. Jesus is not a Democrat or Republican. Christ is above all earthly authorities, and we would do well to remember that. We cannot claim God for our political side. God has no political side. We can assess where the Bible stands on issues of policy and make our decisions, but that is all we can do. Each of us must live with our convictions on the candidates we choose. Let us not be divided over politics or fall prey to the current "patriotic gospel" that has begun to permeate evangelical Christianity.

Overcoming the Danger of Division

The danger of division can come about in many ways, but the result is always the same. When believers choose to battle one another instead of spreading the Gospel message, we damage our witness and create turmoil within the body. Overcoming this danger will often involve putting aside petty complaints or the desire for a "perfect" church body. We may still have folks in our church we don't agree with politically or on other topics, but if the Word of God is preached, and we are growing in our daily walk with Christ, He will take care of our hearts in regard to petty matters.

For those who struggle with letting the little things bother them to the point of causing distress within the body as a whole, go to God in prayer and ask that He help shift focus from these grievances that are most decidedly earthly. It's difficult to complain when our eyes are on Christ. When our eyes are fixed on Jesus, we are not going to be concerning ourselves with what others are doing, which, as it turns out, is very helpful in not letting small things affect us. In some situations, it is more than just simple matters that may cause strife; my emphasis here has been on smaller issues because they are often overlooked, yet they are just as damaging.

I will close with a verse that sums up the nature of division and its effect on the body of believers. I believe the apostle Paul put it best in his first letter to the Corinthian church:

> For the body does not consist of one member but of many. If the foot should say, "Because I am not a hand, I do not belong to the body," that would not make it any less a part of the body. And if the ear should say, "Because I am not an eye, I do not belong to the body," that would not make it any less a part of the body. If the whole body were an eye, where would be the sense of hearing? If the whole body were an ear, where would be the sense of smell? But as it is, God arranged the members in the body, each one of them, as he chose. If all were a single member, where would the body be? As it is, there are many parts, yet one body. The eye cannot say to the hand, "I have no need of you," nor again the head to the feet, "I have no need of you." On the contrary, the parts of the body that seem to be weaker are indispensable, and

on those parts of the body that we think less honorable we bestow the greater honor, and our unpresentable parts are treated with greater modesty, which our more presentable parts do not require. But God has so composed the body, giving greater honor to the part that lacked it, that there may be no division in the body, but that the members may have the same care for one another. (1 Corinthians 12:14–25)

The Danger of Doubt

WHEN WE SEE SOMETHING BAD HAPPEN—OR WHEN SOMETHING occurs in our own lives that we consider tragic—the natural human response seems to be finding somewhere to assign blame. Surely, if innocent people or good folks die or are hurting, someone is to blame.

One of the only times you could likely get the world to acknowledge a Creator God is when He becomes an easy target to blame for the suffering in the world. After all, if God is good and loving, why do all of these bad things happen? Acknowledging God only to blame Him is a preferred practice of many a skeptic. And for the Christian, finding a response to such accusations against God can be difficult. After all, in many instances, Christians may be just as prone to blaming God as the skeptics.

The danger of doubt comes when we feel we're doing all the right things only to have something go wrong in our lives. Christians understand in general that God is not the author of pain and suffering. And we can easily refer to Romans 8:28 to remind us when there is suffering outside of our immediate circumstances that God works all things together for the good of those who love Him:

> And we know that for those who love God all things work together for good, for those who are called according to his purpose. (Romans 8:28)

So, why does it become so easy to doubt God's goodness or love when the circumstances hit closer to home? The danger of doubt, specifically regarding tragic or trying circumstances, is an ever-present danger for which Christians need to be on the lookout. To better understand the age-old question of why bad things happen to good people, we must look at it from the perspective that no one is good apart from Jesus.

We are all born into a fallen world in a fallen state—and even Jesus promised the Christian life would not be easy. That is a big reason for this book. Since we know as Bible-believing Christians that only by the blood of Jesus can we be "good" by God's standard, we need to instead focus on reasons why bad things may be occurring in our lives as believers. If we can recognize God working in our dark times and lean on His promises, then we can avoid this danger of doubt, which has the potential to throw our belief into question.

I would like to borrow some concepts from a great series by Mike Fabarez of Compass Bible Church, "Our Fight with Sin,"[16] and discuss some possible reasons for why believers may be experiencing pain or trouble in their lives. My intention will not be to copy Mike's words verbatim but rather to use the structure he presented as a jumping off point.

Mike presents some compelling possible explanations for Christian hardship. Hardship or bad things happening to a believer could be simple opposition from the world. It could be a consequence of our unconfessed or lingering sin; on a grander scale, it could be the effect of sin on the entirety of creation. It could be testing to prove our saving faith is genuine—or even training for better things to come. Perhaps the hardest for our delicate sensibilities to stomach: it could be the loving discipline of God our Father since we are His adopted sons and daughters in Christ.

The World's Opposition

> If the world hates you, know that it has hated me
> [Jesus] before it hated you. If you were of the world,

---

[16] Fabarez, Mike. "Our Fight with Sin." Focal Point Ministries. September 2, 2007, https://focalpointministries.org/product/our-fight-with-sin-part-1/.

the world would love you as its own; but because you are not of the world … therefore the world hates you. (John 15:18–19)

Jesus's words here tell us it is possible that the pain or trouble we experience as believers is simply a product of the world hating the Savior for which we stand. It could be the ruler of this world, Satan, using his influence over ungodly people and powers to harm those standing for God. I speak more of this in "The Danger of Sacrifice," but a prime example of this would be believers who are persecuted for their beliefs.

We know that of the twelve primary apostles of Jesus, all but John died a martyr's death. The temptation would be, when facing our mortality for the sake of Christ, to doubt God's goodness or develop a "why me?" attitude. In many instances of true persecution, though, the Holy Spirit grants believers the courage to stand for their beliefs in Christ—even unto death—but what about for Christians who are under no immediate threat of death their beliefs in Christ?

Consider Him who endured from sinners [unbelievers] such hostility against himself, so that you may not grow weary or fainthearted. (Hebrews 12:3)

God's Word says oppression from the world is a normal part of the Christian life. However, much of our opposition as Western Christians is in the form of relationship or job loss.

God may put it on your heart to speak up for Christ at your job. Many workplaces might simply warn you in the name of equality, but perhaps your workplace has zero tolerance for speaking out for Christ on a hot-button issue. Now, you're fired. What do you do? What should we as believers do?

First and foremost, we should pray. We can confirm that what happened was indeed simply ungodly opposition to Christ and us by proxy. We are experiencing strife, but in this instance, it is not because of a specific sin or error. Instead, it is a product of sin and the enemy's power as a whole.

God will work it out for us as He has promised to do. Of the possible reasons for pain or suffering in the life of believers, this one is the simplest to grasp. Significant danger of doubt in this instance would likely affect only the newest of believers.

However, perhaps it is another of the considerations for why suffering would occur in the life of a believer. It could be—and this is likely to happen to every true believer at some point—God testing that our faith is genuine.

Testing That Our Faith Is Genuine

God may permit, not bring about, trouble in our lives so that in overcoming the trouble, our faith is proved genuine to not only ourselves but to everyone around us. It will prove that we don't bail out and abandon God the moment the going gets tough—even when it is so tough that we feel we cannot bear it. For my wife, Juliet, and me, this proving of faith occurred during the time between March 19 and March 24, 2013.

The events told here are true, and they are ultimately easier to speak about now that some time has passed. Let the writing used here not in any way diminish the pain and darkness we experienced during that time.

In 2013, we found out that Juliet was pregnant with what would be our first child. We hadn't been trying, but neither were we opposed to having children. And so, with the joy of anticipated new life, we excitedly informed our close family.

The first ultrasound was great, and though it took a moment, we heard the baby's heartbeat and felt that joy rise again. To celebrate, we embarked upon what I affectionately called our pregnancy tour. We first visited Juliet's family in Mexico, and then we headed back to see my family in Oklahoma. We covered all the parents and celebrated the coming of a first grandchild for them. We got back to Austin, ready to begin the next week, on Monday, March 18, 2013.

Monday

My mom had just accepted a position in Austin, Texas, where we were living, and was readying to move from Oklahoma. She would be close by, and that was another great reason to celebrate with a new baby on the way. The plan was for her to stay with us while her husband, Joe, got things prepped to move their RV down from Tulsa to Austin. If memory serves me right, she was going to be staying with us that week. That night, Juliet and I goofed around online using an application to combine our pictures into what a potential baby would look like. We slept, ready for Juliet's eleven-week ultrasound visit to check in on baby's growth.

Tuesday

Juliet was feeling odd on Tuesday, and when the Doppler ultrasound had trouble finding a heartbeat, we were told, at eleven weeks, that was still normal, and we should do the main ultrasound again to get better results. We were encouraged when the ultrasound technician found the baby easily—but she then let us know that she could not find the baby's heartbeat. Our baby had not grown past eight and a half weeks. Juliet's doctor explained that it was nothing we had done wrong and that there was nothing we could have done differently. It was just an unexplained occurrence that was more common than we had realized and affected around one in five pregnancies. We would find out later that many people we knew well had experienced similar situations.

We looked at one another and felt a spiritual sense of calm and peace even in our sorrow. Our lives as believers are not promised to be free of trial, and we accepted God's plan in the baby not surviving. Had that been all that occurred that week, I know we would have healed more quickly, but the week that had begun so joyfully would soon take a turn for the worse.

Wednesday

We went home because Juliet's doctor had said she would miscarry naturally. We informed our family and friends and made a tentative appointment to have a D&C by Friday of the week if the remains of our baby had not yet passed naturally. There was some hesitation regarding this, but knowing the baby was now with Jesus, we accepted that getting Juliet through the miscarriage was our next biggest concern.

Thursday: Juliet's Twenty-Ninth Birthday

Warning: Graphic but necessary explanation ahead.

Neither of us could have predicted what happened on Juliet's birthday that Thursday in 2013. We knew it would be sorrowful but had vowed to try to celebrate anyway. After my mom left for the day to begin training at her new job, we realized Juliet was bleeding. We figured this was just the sad but expected moment of miscarriage. A few moments later, she called me into the bathroom to say the bleeding was not stopping. As I looked at her, I realized she was completely white in the face—and I knew we needed to get her to the ER as soon as possible. God, in a season of great spiritual growth for us, was using a circumstance that would have occurred anyway to test our resolve to lean on Him even during our pain.

We arrived at the ER, and they rushed Juliet off to a room to get her vitals checked and provide care. We spent what felt like hours there with Juliet's blood pressure dropping down to 60/40 at one point and staying quite low otherwise. She was still losing blood steadily during all of this time but had not miscarried completely. I thought a few times that I was going to lose her, and I kept praying that God would spare her and continue to show His faithfulness even in this calamity.

Juliet had not stopped bleeding for what I now remember was about three hours when a nurse finally took action. The D&C that was scheduled for the following day as a tentative thing became immediately necessary if Juliet was going to survive. Her doctor was not available, so they called in another of the hospital's doctors to perform an emergency D&C to try to stop the bleeding. She had lost nearly two pints of blood by that time and ended up needing a blood transfusion.

As they searched for a vein on her arm, missing multiple times, I felt a measure of doubt creeping into my heart. I prayed and knew God was still in control, but the danger of doubting was always present and had to be kept at bay. I was afraid, after losing our baby, that I would now lose my wife as well. If the explanation here does not sound serious, it is my difficulty in expressing just how truly close she came to dying from this bleeding that would not stop.

There was nothing left to do but pray and trust God as they wheeled her into surgery once they had transfused enough blood to get her back to a normal level. It turned out that part of the baby's remains that were holding open some sort of inner part and causing the blood to flow without ceasing.

While she was in surgery, I called and spoke with my dad, updated family, and continued to pray and lean on God to bring us through. The worship leader at our new church came to offer comfort while I waited for the news of her surgery. God had tested that our faith would not give up even in the direst of circumstances, and it proved genuine. Thanks be to God. We ended up staying overnight in the hospital to be safe and formulated how we would announce the sad news to our friends and family.

Through sharing our experience in detail online, many other women reached out to Juliet with similar stories of miscarriages that were beyond their control. We landed on Paul's words in 2 Corinthians 1:3–4:

> Blessed be the God and Father of our Lord Jesus
> Christ, the Father of mercies and God of all comfort,
> who comforts us in all our affliction, so that we may
> be able to comfort those who are in any affliction, with
> the comfort with which we ourselves are comforted
> by God.

Often, trials in the lives of believers have a twofold purpose. It grows and proves our justification while also preparing us to help and empathize with others who may be going through something similar. And in the years since, Juliet has had the opportunity on numerous occasions to help and relate to others who have experienced similar circumstances.

Sunday

Perhaps, to further seal my public acknowledgment and proof of saving faith, God had strategically arranged for baptisms that Sunday, and I saw it as the perfect way to show that we did not lose faith and even glorified God amid our pain.

Around that time, a skeptical friend of mine posted an article called "The God Who Wasn't There." It was poor timing and resulted in a rift that lasted a few years despite our previous close relationship. In reading through it, we saw how utterly incorrect it was about God. He was there in the room with us when we didn't hear the heartbeat. He comforted us and joined us when Juliet was losing blood and when her surgery was successful. And He gave us wisdom and perspective that we shared with our friends—believers and nonbelievers alike— that I believe truly showed faith in action.

God is sovereign over all, and a reliance on that is the only lasting comfort that can be found in tragic times. We keep standing on God's promise that He will never leave or forsake us, His chosen flock. People have said before that Satan tries his hardest to shake a believer's confidence in God as they draw nearer to Him.

We could have cursed God that week or cast blame on Him. It would have been easy, and no doubt many would have agreed with the sentiment. Instead, God decided that week would be a time of maturing as believers, and He wanted my profession of faith in public by baptism to be wholly authentic. Trial and tribulation led to maturity in our walks with Christ. Adversity showed us that we needed help outside of ourselves.

Even in our hardest times as believers, we trust that though sorrow may last for the night, joy in Christ always comes in the morning. I was baptized in front of Juliet and my mom at our church home and emerged from the waters renewed. There was still grieving and pain to work through—and over the years, we have had times of struggle regarding the situation—but we have been able to look back and see God with us every step of the way. And more than any other event experienced in my life, this proved genuine faith in God.

The danger of doubt often hits us hard when we're most vulnerable, but overcoming it in these circumstances brings great victory for believers. Oddly enough, six years to the day from that 2013 week, Juliet ended up in the ER again. Yet thinking back to 2013, I encouraged her in her anxiety. I told her God had already proven faithful in our past times of trial. And all was well. We gave praise to God that though He may test our faith with circumstances that occur from a cursed world, He will also be there with open arms to ease our burdens after the storm has passed.

As we can see, the danger of doubt sometimes attacks with less force than at other times. In instances of testing our faith, it sometimes hits harder than expected and takes all we have to not doubt God's providence in the situation.

The Discipline of a Loving Father

In some instances, and this one is a bit hard to stomach as well, believers may be experiencing discipline from God. He is, after all, our Father when we are adopted into His family by Christ. Delicate sensibilities that see God more as the provider only of blessing and never reproof may find offense here, but the writer of Hebrews states the case well:

> My son, do not regard lightly the discipline of the Lord, nor be weary when reproved by him. (Hebrews 12:5)

Do not be weary. Do not begin to doubt or complain when God reproves us with a trial in our lives—at least not when we can discern whether or not it is discipline. God is our heavenly Father, and we are adopted into His family. And like any good father, when the child disobeys, there is a measure of discipline fitting to the situation.

In his series, Mike likes to call it "spiritual spankings." This seems accurate. I know spanking in our day seems incompatible with culture, but there is value in the discipline of a parent. There is also a purpose. Spiritual discipline from God is not done in a mean-spirited way. It is to teach and grow us as believers, and to help us see that God is our Father who cares deeply for us and our lives.

> "For the Lord disciplines the one he loves and chastises [punishes] every son whom he receives." It is for discipline that you [the believer] have to endure. God is treating you as sons. For what son is there whom his father does not discipline? If you are left without discipline in which all have participated, then you are illegitimate children and not sons. (Hebrews 12:6–8)

The writer of Hebrews explains how if you aren't experiencing a consequence of disobeying God, then you ought to question whether you are a true child of God in Christ. If we are His children, we can expect Him to occasionally discipline us to keep our sanctification moving forward. We can take comfort in this knowing that we are truly saved believers if God disciplines us for outright disobedience of His commands:

He disciplines us for our good, that we may share in his holiness. (Hebrews 12:10)

Are we to doubt God's goodness when we have disobeyed and received a justified consequence for our actions? Surely not. We should thank God that He loves us as a Father and desires the best for us. That is to daily sanctify ourselves and become more like Him, which opens our fellowship and aligns us with His will and purpose for our lives.

If a believer is undergoing suffering, this is the easiest possibility to discern—and either acknowledge the discipline or rule it out as a reason behind the trial. If we are in Christ and sincerely ask if our trials are due to something we've done, He will answer. What father would not explain the reason for a child's punishment? If this is the cause of our pain, and we are truly in Christ, then God will hear us and make it clear so that we can course correct. It may not end the pain, much like a spanking still occurs even when we are told why, but we can adjust.

An important point to clarify here is that this does not in any way mean God is just sitting around waiting for us to mess up so He can punish us. That view is dangerous and not the intention of this explanation if truly grasped. We are forgiven by the blood of Christ, but if we persist as believers in patterns of sin or constantly disobey God's clear commands for us, like a father finally getting up from the couch when the child has ignored him over and over, God may get up to "spiritually spank" us to get us back to where we should be. For an unbeliever, this will seem like we worship a mean God, but this type of correction is meant for our maturity and growth.

God shows His love for us by helping us—no matter how painful—become more like Christ every day. We cannot achieve it in this life, but to be useful in our Christian walks, to hear Him say, "Well done, good and faithful servant" (Matthew 25:21), God may push us along into maturity. And as any child who has received just punishment from their father knows, they learn to respect them and see the love behind it in hindsight.

When we experience trouble in our lives, we can ask God if it is His discipline, and if we truly wait for the answer, He will make it clear by His Holy Spirit. David gave an example of this sort of prayer in Psalm 139 when he wrote:

> Search me, God, and know my heart; test me and know
> my anxious thoughts. See if there is any offensive way
> in me. (Psalm 139:23–24 NIV)

We hope this is not common in our lives as believers. Though we may still sin and fall short, if we are repentant and truly turn away from the sin, this type of correction is rarely needed. Think of it as a kick in the pants that helps to break us out of our sin patterns and grow us in our walks with Christ.

Training for the Big Game

Finally, struggle or pain in the life of a believer may be God training us for something great He has planned. An athlete training for the big game knows that getting prepared to perform at their best can be painful at times. This is different than God testing our faith because God would only train up those who He knows are His. This is God getting us ready to bear more fruit, and this is preparation and practice for a greater purpose He has in store.

> Every branch in me [Jesus] … that does bear fruit
> he [Father God] prunes, that it may bear more fruit.
> (John 15:2)

Now, I don't know a ton about plants, but I do know that pruning involves some trimming away of excess and also some living parts to promote growth. The key here is that even living, healthy portions need trimming at times to grow. I imagine this is not a pleasing process for the plant, but it is to ready the vine to bear even more fruit. As believers, we must understand our goal in this life is not to just get our bodies into the pew every Sunday. God placed us here and called us in Christ for a greater purpose. More often than not, that purpose will require some adjustment in our lives—some pruning.

This is another instance of the pain being purposeful. It is likely meant as training or preparation for a greater ministry that God is calling us into. Do we doubt the need for God to make us bear as much fruit for the kingdom as we can? The pruning may be painful, just as the athlete is sore after practice, but the ultimate goal is preparation for something bigger. God will be our coach as we mature in our faith to better prepare us to do His will for our lives.

This concept reminds me of an experience my mom, LeeAnn, had years ago. She wrote about a time when she truly felt God speaking to her. She wrote down what was said to her heart, and in the morning, she read what it said. It truly had been God guiding her pen. This happened in the midst of a great season of trial for her as a believer. While staying at a Motel 6 for some alone time, she had cried out to God in her desperation. She awoke to what she described as hundreds of lights in the shape of crosses. As she wrote, not seeing what she was writing, this is a bit of what God put on her heart:

> I haven't abandoned you, LeeAnn. I am with you always. You want what is not possible. You cannot live life without struggles and some pain. You will have human struggles, but you will not be alone. I am carrying you. Let Me guide you. Follow My will, not your wants. You must learn to trust in My plan for you. It is My timetable not yours. Be patient and let Me work in your life. Trust Me with your fears and your doubts. I will carry them for you and allow you to be joyful in the knowledge that always you and those you love are in My arms.

She jokingly pointed out that knowing her handwriting, which was pretty bad, it was a small miracle she could even read what she had written the next day. This just confirmed to her that it had been a God moment.

My mom had a life of struggles, yet she always found joy in the midst of them. She knew there was a greater purpose for which God had her in mind. God used her gift for writing and her sense of humor to bless many lives in her sixty-one years on earth. On June 13, 2020, she went home to be with the Lord.

Though her final months had also been a time of great struggle as she battled through mantle cell lymphoma and diabetes, she still wrote about her experiences with a great sense of humor. Even in the struggle, she tried her best to find moments of joy. When she passed from this life to the next, no doubt like her mother before her, she heard Him say, "Well done, good and faithful servant."

As hard as it was to lose her, I know also it was a season of growth for me. It prepared my heart to lean more fully on God as I continue seeking His purpose in my own life. My mom and I were very close, and a good deal of my faith was built upon by her over the years. Her purpose for which God refined her all of her life through both joyful times and trials was fulfilled while she was alive and continues even now after her death.

Overcoming the Danger of Doubt

The danger of doubt is perhaps not as common in mature believers as in those who are newer to the faith. However, in a way, that is really who much of this book is directed to. We only need to read Christ's teaching about picking up our crosses to understand that the life of a Christian is not promised to be free of pain. In fact, in this world, we will have troubles, but in Christ, we don't doubt. We rejoice because He has overcome the world. We are His children. We are growing in righteousness and love of God daily as we seek Him in His Word and go to Him in prayer. Pain and suffering for a believer can be viewed from another perspective than for a nonbeliever, and perspective can ultimately help us see that God is truly working together all things for the good of those who love Him.

> For all who are led by the Spirit of God are sons of God. (Romans 8:14)

> But you have received the Spirit of adoption as sons, by whom we cry "Abba! Father!" The Spirit himself bears witness with our spirit that we are children of God, and if children, then heirs—heirs of God and fellow heirs with Christ, provided we suffer with him in order that we also may be glorified with him. (Romans 8:15–17)

> And we know that for those who love God all things work together for good, for those who are called according to his purpose. For those whom he foreknew, he also predestined to be conformed to the image of his son … And those whom he predestined he also called, and those whom he called he also justified, and those whom He justified he also glorified. (Romans 8:28–30)

God has called believers and justified us in Christ in an instant, securing our future hope with Him. Yet as new creations in Christ, we are compelled to pursue godliness as best as we are able while still in a sin-filled world. Our works do not save us, but as saved children of God, an outpouring of actions and good works naturally flows as evidence of our salvation. God may discipline us, test us, train us, or convict us, but when we are found truly in the faith, it is meant always for our good. And so, we don't give in to doubt or let Satan and the world cause us to question God's goodness during the trials. Instead, we remember God's promise that for those who are called according to His purpose who love Him and seek to obey Him, all things work together for good. How then could the danger of doubt even touch us? If God is for us, who can be against us?

The Danger of Hypocrisy

One of the many dangers of calling ourselves Christians is the type of attention it draws from those outside the faith—and the need to let our actions show that we are set apart from the world, not of it. We are to let our lights shine into a dark world.

Sadly, Christians are often the ones letting the world see darkness. Through hateful speech and behavior toward others, and through not behaving as we are called to do, Christians can very easily give Christ a bad name. Many Christians must face the danger of hypocrisy daily and must strive to show the love of Christ to others:

> If anyone says, "I love God," and hates his brother, he is a liar; for he who does not love his brother whom he has seen cannot love God whom he has not seen. (1 John 4:20)

I understand it is tough in a culture that no longer accepts the Bible believer as a legitimate voice. It can be hard not to be labeled a bigot for not validating the various actions and issues that the culture validates. However, we must strive not to give the world more ammo against us than it already thinks it has. Christians can stand firm on issues that don't align with cultural views if they can do it respectfully. Even though we are new creations in Christ (2 Corinthians 5:17), we know that we are not perfect. Unfortunately, the world outside of Christianity likes to expect perfection from us. Therefore, it is important to clarify the differences between acting hypocritical and being labeled this way unjustly.

Unjustly Labeled

An example of being unjustly labeled would be the controversy with Chick-fil-A back in the summer of 2012. A statement was made by Dan Cathy, the CEO, affirming his stance on traditional, biblical marriage. Because this went against the cultural shift going on at that time, many labeled him a bigot. In this example, a Christian man was unjustly labeled for simply expressing his view on a particular issue.

Those who cry for tolerance are unable to be tolerant themselves if anyone disagrees. We see this happening often these days. Ironically, the outside world then becomes the same hypocrites they accuse the Christians of being. They only tolerate viewpoints that are equivalent to their own while still expecting everyone to validate their viewpoint. As it stands in our culture today, any Christian who affirms a stance that disagrees with the cultural norm may be labeled in such a hateful way, but that really shouldn't surprise us too much.

The danger of hypocrisy is not just the danger of being a hypocrite; there is also the danger of being perceived that way unjustly. The unjust perception comes with the territory of following Christ and is a danger of the faith that one should expect and not take lightly. Christ even used the word hate in describing how the world would see His followers.

> If the world hates you, know that it has hated me before it hated you. (John 15:18)

In some ways, this danger of Christianity will be the hatred that the Christian receives from our culture. Yet, as we will see, we can still love and bring to a knowledge of Christ those who persecute us:

> Bless those who persecute you; bless them and do not curse them. (Romans 12:14)

The wrongful accusation of hypocrisy or hate comes from a confusion of two words: tolerance and validation. The world says Christians are intolerant if they don't accept its behavior hook, line, and sinker. Christians must understand that we can be tolerant of a behavior or issue without validating the behavior.

When the Pharisees brought the woman who committed adultery to stone her, Jesus did not grab His stone too. He did not condemn the woman—and He did not validate her adultery. Jesus told her to sin no more, but He did not throw stones because of her sin. There is a danger for Christians to be more like the Pharisees in these situations. Too often, we get up in arms and try to verbally or emotionally stone the person in sin or of a certain lifestyle. At this point, we become intolerant and even hateful, and the world sees us this way. If we become those wishing to throw stones, we validate the world's opinion of us and prove ourselves to be hateful. When we do not condemn but rather leave the judgment in God's hands, we respect the person without validating the sin. Then if we are still called intolerant, it is a wrongful accusation. In the danger of hypocrisy, it is better to be wrongfully accused than to truly be hypocritical in our actions.

We have our own sins, and to stone someone over a sin we perceive as greater than our own is an act of hypocrisy in itself. This is the type of hypocrisy we need to avoid in our walks with Christ. We do not have to support or validate the sin, but we can treat the person as a valued human while encouraging them to leave the sin. Though, biblically, it is not for us to judge those outside the faith.

> For what have I to do with judging outsiders? Is it not those inside the church whom you are to judge? God judges those outside. "Purge the evil from among you." (1 Corinthians 5:12–13)

Paul says we are to hold other believers accountable and make right judgments within the body—but not to judge the outside world because God has that under control. Too many Christians begin to give Christ a bad name by passing judgment and condemnation on those outside the faith. Often, this only serves to push a person further from Christ and deeper into sin.

We can stand firm in God's Word, but not automatically condemn those who are not aligned unless they are in the church. Even then, there is a process for it, and we want to be respectful of our brothers and sisters in the faith. We must love our worldly neighbors as much as our Christian brothers and sisters:

> Do you suppose, O man—you who judge those who practice such things, and yet do them yourself—that you will escape the judgment of God? (Romans 2:3)

The world can sometimes mislabel us. In that sense, we are usually doing something correctly. Christ brought division because His life and teachings were radically different than others of that day. What about when the Christian deserves the label of hypocrite? As we will see, there is still a danger of actually being a hypocrite within the faith.

Actually Hypocritical

I've often heard from non-Christians that their reason for not going to church or believing is because of all the hypocrisy in the church. My typical response is this, "Yes, the church is full of people seeking Christ who may have been sinning the week before, but not following Christ because of someone else's actions fails to acknowledge that we are individually accountable to God. Using the behavior of others as an excuse for not believing does not free anyone from that accountability."

This excuse always reminds me of someone saying they won't go to a gym because there are out of shape people inside. Anyone coming to Christ must first look hypocritical on the surface because the act of turning from our sin to faith itself is an experience of two extremes. Are we to judge the alcoholic who stumbles into church on Sunday and prays for forgiveness because the night before he was on a bender? I think not. The world may judge and not understand, but we should be welcoming to all who would seek Christ.

In Luke's Gospel, we see the hypocrisy of the Pharisees who were the religious people of their day; they were the legalistic churchgoers, if you will. We see them praying and thanking God that they are not like the sinful people such as robbers or tax collectors (a shameful occupation in that day).

In the prayer, the Pharisee rattles off his list of religious accomplishments to God, but a tax collector is also there praying:

> But the tax collector stood at a distance. He would not even look up to heaven, but beat his breast and said, "God have mercy on me, a sinner." (Luke 18:13 NIV)

Christ continues with His example and explains that it is the tax collector who is justified in his prayer because he prayed in humility and with a spirit of repentance. Many church members today are more like the Pharisee in this parable than the tax collector, and that is a danger. We must never forget that no matter how faithful we are in our walks, we also were once sinners in need of mercy.

The outside world sees the church as a place of condemnation, and in reality, though we stand in the truth of God's Word, we are to love our neighbors, before, after, and even if they never believe. The excuse of the nonbeliever to not go to church because of hypocrites would not be an issue if Christians could avoid the danger of open sin on Saturday with church and piety on Sunday. We will fail, yes, and Christ is faithful to forgive us then, but we must strive to be Christians not only in word but also in action.

From Monday at the office to Sunday in the pew, we need to love as Christ loved and live as Christ lived to the best of our abilities that we may not give anyone reason to truthfully call us hypocrites. Let false accusations abound if they must, but let it not be said we have become actual hypocrites. Live lives that glorify God all week long.

Hate

Another danger for Christians is falling into the trap of hate toward others because of a disagreement in belief. The Westboro

Baptist "Church" is one of the prime contributors of the past two decades of painting Christians as hateful, bigoted people. And the fact a congregation of only about forty people can give Christians such a bad name shows the damaging power of Christians who hate.

I understand a firm stance on issues of fundamental importance, but the way Christians approach a viewpoint on an issue can say a lot about their hearts. The deliberate hate and attacks on Christians and non-Christians alike should demonstrate easily that Westboro is not following Christ's teaching. Sadly, they easily grab headlines, and the perceived hypocrisy of all Christians—whether hateful or not—gets brought back to the spotlight.

Jesus gives the command to love one another as He loved us (John 13:34). And sinful or not, He first loved us and called us out of our sin. He did not picket the prostitution house; He ate in fellowship and respect with sinners while still not validating that way of life.

While some Christians may love so much they forget to share God's truth, love is still an important aspect of the Gospel as a whole:

> Let us love one another, for love is from God, and whoever loves has been born of God, and knows God ... because God is love ... In this is love, not that we have loved God but that he loved us and sent his Son to be propitiation for our sins. (1 John 4:7, 9–10)

> Above all, keep loving one another earnestly, since love covers a multitude of sins. (1 Peter 4:8)

In John's epistle and his Gospel account, we see love manifest in much of his writing. However, John was originally known as a "Son of Thunder" because of his behavior when he first began following Christ. James, another of Jesus's closest disciples, was also known by this nickname. We see, however, that as they grew in Christ and followed Him, they became filled more with love than hate. Christ transformed their hot tempers to love. The example of how they behaved before can be seen in chapter 9 of Luke's Gospel account:

And he sent messengers ahead of him [Jesus], who went and entered a village of Samaritans to make preparations for him [Jesus]. But the people did not receive him, because his face was set toward Jerusalem. And when his disciples James and John saw it, they said, "Lord, do you want us to tell fire to come down from heaven and consume them?" But he turned and rebuked them. (Luke 9:52–55)

James and John, the "Sons of Thunder," were two of Jesus's three closest disciples, yet in that verse, they appeared to be more like Westboro wanting to call down fire on the unbelievers. Jesus rebuked them because His path is of bringing repentance through love—not anger or hate. John and James both went on to have a strong spirit for discernment, but they tempered it with love after walking with Christ. In the same way, Christians must speak the truth in essential elements of the faith—but always temper our speech with love so that the light of Christ and His teaching might still show through us.

Politics

We have seen how the danger of hypocrisy and hate can manifest through our behavior as Christians and how it can be easy to be on fire for God and forget we aren't here to call down fire from God. Let's look at one more common area in which many Christians struggle not to give Christ a bad name: the sphere of religion and politics.

With an ever-changing political climate, it can be difficult for Christians to remain unpolarized. Our culture likes polarization, and people are either part of the left or the right. And in the sense that one side aligns with our personal beliefs, it is okay to lean in one direction or the other. However, disagreements stemming from political discussions can have a damaging effect on our witnesses for Christ if we get too caught up in choosing sides.

Jesus was not more liberal or more conservative by our strict definitions today, and Christians do well to remember this. We do not want to make our brethren look bad—or the faith as a whole look bad or hypocritical—when Christians spend all of their energy arguing with other Christians over political matters.

We must remember that whether Democrat or Republican, Independent, or other, political candidates are where they are by God's will in His sovereign knowledge. We might not always see a direct reason for this, but biblically speaking, we ought to remember it:

> Let every person be subject to the governing authorities. For there is no authority except from God, and those that exist have been instituted by God. Therefore, whoever resists the authorities resists what God has appointed, and those who resist will incur judgment. (Romans 13:1–2)

Paul's writing here has always seemed to me to be a good, cut-and-dried view for Christians to take. However, too often—especially in this time of heavy social media use—Christians pick a side and then bash the other or deny the governing leaders' authority. Peter also brings this up in a briefer fashion in his first epistle:

> Honor everyone. Love the brotherhood. Fear God. Honor the emperor. (1 Peter 2:17)

Biblically speaking, Christians must accept God's sovereignty on the matter. The fact we have terms like "fundamentalist" and "Christian right" is because Christians have become too antagonistic in their political views. This often paints them as hateful or rebellious, which causes division with the world and division within the faith—and it is quite easy to fall into this divisive behavior.

Overcoming this political dissension might be one of the easier things to do as Christians if we simply take the Bible at its word as we claim to do. When it comes to avoiding the danger of infighting or painting Christ into a corner, I suggest we focus on two specific mind-sets in our politics. First, focus on relevant personal issues. I would define a relevant personal issue as something in the political realm that has a direct, immediate effect on an individual's way of life.

For example, I have an active interest in immigration policy and reform because my wife is originally from Mexico, and we have had to deal directly with that arduous process. Now, as a Christian, I must remember that by having an issue close to my heart, there may be a tendency to get fired up about it. Stating facts or correcting an opposing view in love are not inherently bad, but I cannot fight other Christians who may disagree with my stance. I may have to support a candidate with whom I don't agree 100 percent if their stance on my relevant personal issue is aligned with my own.

Secondly, we focus on candidate support. This area is much more difficult for some and is a primary reason why so much discord is sown within the faith and even between Christians and the culture. When a Christian so adamantly opposes another candidate that they become hateful to anyone supporting the candidate, the light of Christ does not shine forward in them.

When they bash and attack an elected candidate—ignoring Paul's words in Romans 13 to do so—they also fall into the danger of hypocrisy and hate. This became apparent to me in recent years when conservative friends bashed Barack Obama for eight years. Now, liberal friends turn around and bash Donald Trump. It is hypocritical of both sides if we are calling ourselves Christians. If unbelievers want to argue about politics back and forth, we really can't help that, but as Christians, we need to engage our brethren on either side of the political spectrum with respect. We can't just be friendly to others when our preferred candidate or political party is in office.

In terms of presidential elections in the United States, there will never be a perfect candidate because candidates are human, whether or not they claim to follow Christian beliefs. Paul and Peter say we must still respect their authority. Christ said to render unto Caesar what is his (Matthew 22:17–21) because, in God's sovereign plan, He has placed leaders where they are for a reason. The only exception to this rule would be if an individual in power directly (physically) persecutes and targets Christians as a group.

Though we see some of this on a lighter level here in the United States, so far, no president has issued orders for beheading or killing of Christians. At that point, we must remember that, though rulers have authority for a time on earth, God is the ultimate authority. Christians are truly citizens of heaven from the time of their conversion to Christ and must ultimately choose His truth over the truth of earthly rulers:

> But our citizenship is in heaven, and from it we await
> a Savior, the Lord Jesus Christ. (Philippians 3:20)

Again, I clarify, this would primarily be in an instance of direct persecution of Christians by a ruler, similar to what is happening in the Middle East with the beheading of Christians. David writes in Psalm 109 in regard to a persecuting ruler:

> May his days be few, may another take his office ...
> For he did not remember to show kindness but pursued
> the poor and needy ... and put them to death. (Psalm
> 109:8, 16)

In *The Treasury of David*, renowned theologian Charles Spurgeon writes,

> We wish well to all mankind, and for that very reason
> we sometimes blaze with indignation against the
> inhuman wretches by whom every law which protects
> our fellow creatures is trampled down, and every
> dictate of humanity is set at naught.[17]

Politically, Christians should not cause division by arguing over issues with which other Christians may disagree. Accept the

---

[17] Spurgeon, Charles. Treasury of David. (Peabody, MA: Hendrickson Publishing, 1988), 468–474.

differences of opinion in love since political views are almost certainly in the category of nonessential belief with regard to Christian doctrine. We can pray and hope for a Christ follower in office, but we must still respect the authorities appointed by God—even if they are not godly in all their actions.

Overcoming the Danger of Hypocrisy

To address the danger of hypocrisy, our most important weapon is love. We can love those around us so that we are not known for our hate. We must love one another within the faith and not let disagreements paint the faith as a whole in a bad light. Our conversion by faith saved us, but once we enter into following Christ, our actions become the standard by which others can measure the light of Christ within us—and by which we can draw the world by that light.

We are not saved by our works, but our actions can speak volumes about who Christ is and why the world needs Him. As James, a former "Son of Thunder," said in his epistle:

> Be doers of the word, and not hearers only, deceiving yourselves. For if anyone is a hearer of the word and not a doer, he is like a man who looks intently at his natural face in a mirror. For he looks at himself and goes away and at once forgets what he was like. (James 1:22–24)

Let us not forget who we are in Christ and let that light shine to those around us. Let us not fall into the danger of hypocrisy or hatred for those around us. Like the title of an old song says, "They'll know we are Christians by our love."

The Danger of Idolatry

In modern America, we have access to a plethora of options for nearly everything we do. We can go eat at restaurants serving all manner of foods or stay at home and flip through more than six hundred channels of television. We surround ourselves with entertainment and things that satisfy our human desires, but we often forget to encourage and satisfy our spiritual needs.

When we are saved and justified in Christ, the Holy Spirit enters us as believers and begins to work on our hunger for the things of God. If we continue feeding this hunger, daily seeking God in prayer and our Bibles, we grow and mature in the faith. If we begin to put too many of the world's entertainments and temptations into our new Christian lives, then, like weeds, those things begin to choke out our spiritual growth and leave us starved and stagnant in our walks with Christ.

Admittedly, this is a temptation into which many Christians, including myself, have fallen. When we give in to this danger of putting earthly activities and entertainment above our spiritual growth, we can quite easily fall into the danger of idolatry. Though we may not be carving statues to worship or making golden calves, we still symbolically turn our earthly desires into idols of worship. And without fully realizing it, we then let our idols choke out that original hunger for God's Word that was present at our conversion.

To overcome this danger is difficult once we have fallen away from habitually seeking God. We create a nearly impenetrable barrier for ourselves. From that point, we must fight the temptation to remain idolatrous and diligently seek our way back to God. To address this danger of idolatry further, we must also establish at what point something we do or are entertained by becomes an idol to us. I would submit that we create an idol for ourselves when that activity or desire outweighs our desire to seek and serve Christ and to grow in our Christian walks.

Symbolic Idolatry (Entertainment Idols)

The apostle Paul associated covetousness with idolatry. In a way, modern Christians often enter into this covetousness when a desire for things they do not possess causes their hearts to focus on the acquisition of those things above all else:

> Put to death therefore what is earthly in you: sexual immorality, impurity, passion, evil desire, and covetousness, which is idolatry. (Colossians 3:5)

> Therefore, my beloved, flee from idolatry. (1 Corinthians 10:14)

It may seem harmless to be impressed by our neighbor's new flat-screen television. Typically, just admiring or acknowledging the object is not going to cause harm to us. However, when we begin to desire our own even better TV to impress that neighbor or fulfill that desire to have it, we become covetous, and by proxy, idolatrous. The television becomes an idol to us, and we might not always realize this is happening.

This ties back to the initial seeking of earthly things over the things of God. As modern-day Western Christians, we do not likely struggle with literally worshipping idols. We also do not deal directly with the eating of food knowingly sacrificed to idols daily as the early church often did. An exception, perhaps, is the idea of the statues of Buddha found in many Chinese restaurants. While I doubt the cooks are sacrificing the meat to these decorative statues, they could technically be considered a modern-day version of eating food sacrificed to idols. But as Paul points out in his first letter to the Corinthian church:

> "An idol is nothing at all in the world" … For even if there are so-called gods, whether in heaven or on earth … yet for us there is but one God, the Father, from whom all things came and for whom we live; and there is but one Lord, Jesus Christ, through whom all things came and through whom we live. (1 Corinthians 8:4b–6 NIV)

Our modern-day idols are more symbolic and often only become idols because of our intense focus on them. They are not wooden images but activities or desires for which we give the majority of our focus, sacrificing focus that could be spent diligently seeking to grow in our Christian walks.

I've used television as an example, but I am not out to demonize watching TV as a whole by any means. I am not here to question our preferred viewing activity on television, but if it becomes the sole focus of our days, it may be considered a form of idolatry. When we seek the word of the TV, video game, or even another book over the Word of God, we may become idolaters.

Although we are forgiven by the precious blood of Christ, we do ourselves and His sacrifice a disservice by failing to seek Him and grow in our daily walks. I will admit that I am also guilty of this idolatry more often than I'd like to be. Perhaps I use television as a primary example of this danger in the Christian walk because I need to convict the readers of this—and myself. For me, the danger of idolatry is always present and real, and for those wishing to follow Christ, it is a danger of which we must all be aware to remain vigilant.

Life Idols

It is also possible to become so focused on our careers or family lives that we ignore God and our Christian growth to the point of creating symbolic idolatry out of these things. While seeking fulfillment in our career and even financial security is a responsible activity, we must also be careful to balance this pursuit with our pursuit of God and His purpose for us. Are we focused more on the almighty dollar than the Almighty? Do we spend the majority of our time at the office, sacrificing time with God or with family for our careers? These may be red flags that our careers are becoming idols.

For me, this has never really been an issue. I enjoy my job most days, but I realize my true purpose may be found outside of my chosen career path. Therefore, I use the job primarily to pay bills and support my family while trying to pursue passions on my own time. If anything, I may give too little focus to my job in comparison with my time given to personal pursuits and family. Remember that a work-life balance is a balance. If work or life begins to tip the scale too far to one side, we must adjust accordingly.

In keeping our "life idols" at bay, balance is key. I've heard the thought from a few people that if we consider our time spent with God as though He is our spouse—as the Bible says, Christ is the groom and we are His bride—can we expect to deepen in our relationship if we're only engaging with our spouses once a week? Once a month? Of course not! Our time spent with God should be equal to or greater than our time spent on other pursuits—even career and family pursuits.

Obsession

Recently, I became somewhat obsessed with fixing an old iMac computer, mostly because it was working fine before a silly mistake I made rendered it nearly useless. Knowing it had been working at one time, I wanted to get it fixed, and not being able to do it, was driving me nuts. It was a daily thought that invaded as I sat around thinking about what I hadn't tried yet to fix it. I knew basically what was wrong, but I didn't have the resources to fix it. I was also not willing to sell other things I enjoyed having just for a chance to repair this old computer.

One day, while mulling all of this over, God led me to a story in Genesis:

> Once when Jacob was cooking stew, Esau came in from the field, and he was exhausted. And Esau said to Jacob, "Let me eat some of that red stew, for I am exhausted!" (Therefore, his name was called Edom.) Jacob said, "Sell me your birthright now." Esau said, "I am about to die; of what use is a birthright to me?" Jacob said, "Swear to me now." So, he swore to him and sold his birthright to Jacob. Then Jacob gave Esau bread and lentil stew, and he ate and drank and rose and went his way. Thus, Esau despised his birthright. (Genesis 25:29–34)

Obviously, my situation isn't completely the same, but much like Esau with Jacob, I had become exhausted with the need to repair that computer. And like Jacob, the internet was quite happy to offer me a variety of solutions if only I would pay them. And much like the stew, it would only be a temporary relief. It might not work at all and would end up as a loss of time and money.

I believe that I have a bit of obsessive-compulsive disorder. It has not been officially diagnosed, but it feels like it's there. I develop an obsession about doing something and can't mentally rest until it's completed. That's why I don't like when Juliet tells me something at home isn't working properly. If I can't fix it quickly, it becomes my obsession to fix it. I get grumpy and am unable to function at other tasks until it's resolved.

In the story, Jacob was not being the best brother by telling Esau he couldn't eat unless he gave something of value to him first. Since there weren't Burger Kings, it's not like Esau had much more in the way of food options. And if he was truly famished, Jacob could have been a bit more understanding.

However, the way I read it—when thinking of my obsession about things—is that Esau was possibly overreacting. Was there no other food available? Would Jacob have let his brother starve? Couldn't Esau ask his mom to whip up some spaghetti?

What this looked like to me as I read through the story more was Esau becoming so focused on something he wanted that it became an obsession for him. Giving away something of huge value in that day and time was his resolution. Yet right afterward, he regretted it.

Really, how much mental effort was my iMac repair worth? I was giving up time with God for sure, but I was also giving up time with family, monetary resources, and sanity in an attempt to find the solution that would make it work. After exhausting all possible efforts, I decided to cast off the obsession, and I ended up selling it to someone on eBay who had the time and means to pore into it further.

What are you obsessing over? What want has become so forefront in your mind you've made it a need? Have you made an idol out of it as I did with the iMac and my obsession over it? Dwelling so much on the situation had the potential to become sin for me, and it did for a time. I sacrificed resources and time for it.

My intention felt noble. It had been my grandma's old computer—never used—and it was perfect for Hannah to play some games or goof around on for fun. It was a neat item. How important was that? Was it interfering with my daily time with God? With family time? With work time? With my mental well-being? Yes, to all of the above!

> Do not love the world or the things in the world. (1 John 2:15–17)

> But each person is tempted when he is lured and enticed by his own desire. Then desire when it has conceived gives birth to sin, and sin when it is fully grown brings forth death. (James 1:14–15)

Esau could have used some time to contemplate how important the tasty stew was in the grand scheme of things. And compared to what he was giving up, he may have realized how silly that trade was going to be.

I think the key to overcoming obsession practically is perspective, which means taking a step back to analyze how important the task or object we obsess over actually is. Perhaps it means making a list of pros and cons. How will pursuing this affect our relationships and our well-being in general?

I gained perspective by stepping back and from the insight provided by this helpful Bible story. I'm sure the prompting of the Holy Spirit brought it to my attention for that very reason. Don't make an idol of something by obsessing over it.

God's Law and Idolatry

We've seen how we can make idols out of everyday objects by coveting them or dedicating more time to them than to God. Let's consider how idolatry like this looked when God handed down the original law, and in doing so, we can learn how to overcome the temptation of spiritual idolatry.

While Moses was on the mountain with God, receiving His commandments, the people in the camp got impatient and eventually figured he wasn't coming back. So, Aaron, whom Moses had left in charge, bent to the will of the crowd and created an idol. He made a golden calf to worship as a representation of God.

God, aware of what was going on, basically told Moses He was going to wipe the people out because of it (justifiably). Moses interceded on their behalf, and God relented for the sake of Moses and sent him down to address the situation:

> And he [Aaron] received the gold from their hand and fashioned it with a graving tool and made a golden calf. (Exodus 32:4)

Then later, while explaining the action to Moses:

> So I [Aaron] said to them, "Let any who have gold take it off." So they gave it to me, and I threw it into the fire, and out came this calf. (Exodus 32:24)

We just read prior in verse 4 of the same chapter that Aaron had fashioned the calf using tools and molded it. When Moses arrived and asked Aaron what the deal was, Aaron told him that he had thrown the gold into a fire, and when a calf magically appeared, they worshipped it.

Aaron created an idol to appease the impatient people. They had seen God's wonders firsthand, yet when the time came to wait on His plan and His purpose for them, they got tired of waiting and went their own way. This was spiritual and physical idolatry. They made a literal idol to take the place of God. They didn't trust His power and promise; they wanted a physical object to worship. And when confronted with their sin, they attempted to defend it.

How often are we this same way? We know we've sinned, yet when we are confronted, we think of an excuse or try to defend the sin or lessen its severity by explaining it away. God forgives us when we repent, but to repent is to acknowledge and confess our sin before God and show remorse for our actions. We should not try to justify it to God or to others.

Passing the blame for doing wrong was nothing new in Aaron's day. Adam, the first man, did the same thing shortly after he sinned. He allowed Eve to eat the forbidden fruit without stopping her, and he blamed God for creating Eve in the first place as an excuse for his own eating of the fruit.

When God confronts Adam, he says something along the lines of this: "The woman You gave me made me do it!" (Genesis 3:12)

Wow, Adam! You're going to blame God on that one? The chain of reasoning there is basically that God created woman, the woman ate the forbidden fruit, and the man didn't stop her and participated.

However, he blamed God for creating the woman because if she hadn't been created, he wouldn't have sinned.

Sometimes, that chain of logic is exactly what we do as Christians. We like to stay in a more toddler-like state of maturity in Christ. I have a toddler, and it would be just like Hannah—or any toddler—to try to invent some fanciful story to explain something they did wrong. Consider my hypothetical scenario:

Dad: Hannah, did you hit your friend?
Hannah: No, Dada. I was standing here with my fist out and she walked into it. Dad: …
Hannah: That's what happened—she walked into my fist.

We are saved and justified before God in an instant when we come to Christ, but that is just the beginning of a life in which we continually seek to grow and mature in our relationships and knowledge of Christ. Yes, it is true that if we confess our sins, He is faithful to forgive and cleanses us of unrighteousness (1 John 1:9). However, in the very next sentence, John writes,

If we say we have not sinned, we make him a liar, and his word is not in us. (1 John 1:10)

We cannot expect to be forgiven if we're simply denying our sin instead of repenting of it. In the first moment of confrontation, Aaron and Adam both essentially said they didn't sin. Ultimately, both repented and were renewed in fellowship with God—as we also will be. However, if we are to grow and mature as Christians, we need to have the adult reaction of taking responsibility, admitting guilt, and accepting whatever consequence that may entail. Then we move on, not seeking to sin. We confess it and admit our guilt, knowing that by His precious blood, we are forgiven and made whole again in our relationship with Christ. We must not put ourselves in a position to worship something other than God, yet if we do, we must repent and willingly accept our responsibility in the act.

Overcoming the Danger of Idolatry

My life has been punctuated with the high points of theological study and a hunger for God's Word—but nearly equally punctuated with the valleys and deserts of lack of focus and an over interest in the entertainment of the world. Generally, I have been pulled out of these valleys by the mercy of God, and my focus has been renewed. The sanctification of a Christian walk was not promised to be without its difficulties:

> Therefore, my beloved, as you have always obeyed, so now, not only as in my presence but much more in my absence, work out your own salvation with fear and trembling, for it is God who works in you, both to will and to work for his good pleasure. (Philippians 2:12–13)

To turn back from the danger of idolatry, Christians must first admit that we have—however unintentionally—made an idol out of something. We then must fight within to overcome the false sense of contentment given to us by the idol to find the real power and contentment of our relationship with Christ and the study of His Word.

Pastor Matt White of Calvary Worship Center in Austin, Texas, discussed the trend of adults playing Pokémon Go in a blog post: "Pokémon Goes to Church." He makes a good point that I think is applicable to anything that Christians turn into idols:

> Some become so obsessed with the game and games like it that it consumes all or most of their free time.

Rather than pursuing God's purpose and destiny they are allowing these time eaters to devour their life.[18]

This statement sums up well the types of harm caused by the danger of idolatry in the Christian walk. As with the other dangers mentioned in other writings, new Christians must "count the cost" (Luke 14:25–33) of discipleship and the Christian life. With so many distractions surrounding us, this can become a daily struggle. We may even realize that we have idolized something, yet still feel powerless to pull away from its power over our attention.

In my own experience, I find the combination of three things to be most effective in gradually overpowering the pull of something we have made into an idol. First, we must seek God's help in prayer. Confessing our part in the creation of such an idol and our regret over its distraction in our lives is a place to start:

> No temptation has overtaken you that is not common to man. God is faithful, and he will not let you be tempted beyond your ability, but with the temptation he will also provide the way of escape, that you may be able to endure it. (1 Corinthians 10:13)

Second, we must seek God in His Word daily. Our study of the knowledge God imparts to us in His Word and draws our hearts and minds to the things that please Him. When we are immersed in His Word, the Holy Spirit renews our hunger for it—and we become focused on seeking the meat of the Bible over worldly distractions.

Growing up at our church camp, we used to have what we called "TAG time." TAG stands for "time alone with God" and involves finding a location where we are least likely to be distracted as we engage in prayer and the study of God's Word. Seeking this TAG time can help us overcome the danger of idolatry.

---

[18] White, Matthew. "Pokémon Goes to Church," July 26, 2016, http://pastormattwhite.blogspot.com/2016/07/pokemon-goes-to-church.html.

Consider these verses about the importance of the Word of God and our study of it:

All Scripture is breathed out by God and profitable for teaching, for reproof, for correction, and for training in righteousness, that the man of God may be competent, equipped for every good work. (2 Timothy 3:16–17)

Your Word is a lamp to my feet and a light to my path. (Psalm 119:105)

But his delight is in the law of the Lord, and on His law, he meditates day and night. (Psalm 1:2)

Like newborn infants, long for the pure spiritual milk, that by it you may grow up into salvation. (1 Peter 2:2)

How can a young man keep his way pure? By guarding it according to your word. With my whole heart I seek you; let me not wander from your commandments! I have stored up your word in my heart, that I might not sin against you. (Psalm 119:9–11)

Third, we must not neglect gathering as often as we can with our brothers and sisters in Christ. We must encourage one another to grow in Christ and work out our sanctification:

But if we walk in the light, as he is in the light, we have fellowship with one another, and the blood of Jesus his Son cleanses us from all sin. (1 John 1:7)

Again I say to you, if two of you agree on earth about anything they ask, it will be done for them by my Father in heaven. For where two or three gathered in my name, there am I among them. (Matthew 18:19–20)

And let us consider how to stir up one another to love and good works, not neglecting to meet together, as is the habit of some, but encouraging one another, and all the more as you see the Day drawing near. (Hebrews 10:24–25)

With prayer, God's Word, and our brothers and sisters in Christ, we can enter into the Christian life armed against the danger of idolatry. It takes effort, and it does not come easily in our modern culture, but by the grace of God, we will be able to overcome in Christ Jesus.

The Danger of Sacrifice

SPEAKING ABOUT THE DANGER OF SACRIFICE IS ONE OF THE MORE difficult topics to cover regarding the dangers of the Christian faith. If we're honest, no one truly wants to sacrifice anything. On a smaller level, we wince at the thought of losing certain physical comforts or securities in our lives. And if we were to lose physical comforts, at least we would still have relationships with those closest to us.

What if truly taking up our crosses and following Christ involved the loss of relationships as well? And most difficult to consider, though perhaps less of a worry in the Western church, is the ever-present possibility that we may have to give our lives for the sake of Christ. Addressing the danger of sacrifice, however uncomfortable, is necessary for preparing ourselves to grow in our relationships with Christ and to confidently call ourselves Christians.

I don't like the idea of sacrifice any more than others, but at least we have other brothers and sisters in Christ with whom we can share these possibilities. For this section, let's start smaller and work our way up in terms of what sacrifices we may make for Christ.

Physical Comforts

When we think about comforts in our lives, there are likely several things we could rattle off, especially as Christians in the United States. There are, of course, physical comforts on a smaller scale like having internet, electricity, and hot water. Then, there are needs on a larger scale like shelter and food. At the heart of these comforts is the need to work to afford them or maintain them.

As much as I may not like to admit a job is a comfort, it is certain that I am reliant on it to provide for other needs. Some people love what they do, and others simply get by for the next paycheck, but we can't deny money is needed to maintain a level of comfort in life. We don't need to be rich or even love money, but we do need a certain amount to be what many consider comfortable.

I've had the opportunity to travel often to Mexico because of my wife, and it is always humbling to see the hard work and dedication some of the less fortunate there put forth to maintain even the simplest of comforts. In some ways, it's no different than the United States, and many families still have internet, hot water, and electricity. Others live in small casitas with minimal access to modern amenities.

From participating in mission trips to build casitas, I have learned that the families who have the least in terms of physical comforts are the often happiest. There is something to be said about having our basic needs met and getting by on less. The danger of sacrifice, in regard to comforts we may give up for Christ, will not sound as bad as it might to a well-to-do Christian person with a steady income and all the modern comforts.

If we're honest, we often get very attached to a standard of living and are wary of anything that would create a loss of this standard. It reminds me of the story of the rich young ruler in the book of Matthew:

> Jesus said to him, "If you would be perfect, go, sell what you possess and give to the poor, and you will have treasure in heaven; and come, follow me." When the young man heard this he went away sorrowful, for he had great possessions. (Matthew 19:21–22)

The context of this story is that the rich man asks what he must do to receive eternal life. Jesus perceives he is looking for a simple item he can check off of a to-do list and engages him in conversation.

He tells him something true, but which in our flawed human thinking seems like a simple matter. He said to follow the commandments of God.

The man confidently tells Jesus he has always kept the commandments. Eternal life seems within his grasp if it was based on works, but when Jesus points out that only God is good, He pokes a hole in the man's thought process. We know in Christ, it is nothing we do to earn eternal life, but that we have faith in what Christ did for us. In having this belief, we are saved.

Good works should outpour from this, but we are not saved by our works. The rich man wants to inherit eternal life by his works, which is similar to all the other religious systems outside of Christianity. So, as an added challenge, Jesus tells the man to give away all he has and to follow Him. This proves too much for the man who has many earthly comforts and possessions.

The man valued eternal life only as much as it didn't interfere with his creature comforts. He had great possessions, as the verse says, and thinking of the cost of following Jesus, he decided it was too much. He was unable to sacrifice what was needed to wholly trust in Jesus. I don't believe this verse is saying every Christian needs to go sell what they own now and give it away. That would be taking it to an extreme.

Jesus is illustrating that we cannot be ruled by our comforts or our possessions. This man missed out on a greater treasure because he was unwilling to sacrifice the temporary things:

> Do not lay up for yourselves treasures on earth, where moth and rust destroy and where thieves break in and steal, but lay up for yourselves treasures in heaven, where neither moth nor rust destroys and where thieves do not break in and steal. For where your treasure is, there your heart will be also. (Matthew 6:19–21)

And so, the danger of sacrifice may affect us in this same way.

God may call us to step out of a steady job in faith for something better He has planned. He may put on our hearts to give up something that we hold dear for someone more in need than us.

As we mature in our walks with Christ, the Holy Spirit will stir within our hearts the purpose for which God has us in mind. He may do it so profoundly that we can do nothing except step into it on faith or disregard it at our ultimate loss. Growing in our purpose for God will always involve the loss of comfort in some way.

Oddly enough, as I write this book, I'm struggling with the very idea of taking a step of faith in having it published. What about the cost? What about the unknown? What if nothing comes of it—or, worse, what if I've misinterpreted God's purpose and wasted time and resources?

This is exactly the position God likes us to be in when He is about to do a great work. I cannot deny that pursuing this writing—and its ultimate goal of helping my brothers and sisters in Christ understand what they are getting into when they commit to following Jesus—has been on my heart for some time. It has been at least four years in the making—perhaps more by the time it's done—mostly because I doubted myself and did not take the steps of faith God impressed upon me. But, often in the discomfort, God works best.

When the disciples saw Jesus walking on water and Peter asked if he could come to Him on the water, Jesus simply says, "Come." At that point, Peter has a direct word and steps out on faith, which initially goes well. Yet the wind—like the worry in all of our hearts when we step out on faith—crept in and he began to sink. But Jesus caught him.

Jesus will catch us if we step out in God's will for our lives. For every comfort we may sacrifice for Jesus, we understand that we store up treasure in heaven, and potentially even in this life, as we grow in the Lord's purpose. Could we still preach the good news if we didn't have electricity? Of course! Will God take care of us if we lose our jobs? Absolutely. If we are pursuing His will for our lives, and truly in Christ and seeking to grow, He will catch us if we fall and encourage us to move forward. This should be a comfort to us.

We may sacrifice small comforts, but the result with God is always better than the prior situation. Jesus spoke about the care God has for His own in Matthew's Gospel:

> Therefore I tell you, do not be anxious about your life, what you will eat or what you will drink, nor about your body, what you will put on. Is not life more than food, and the body more than clothing? Look at the birds of the air: they neither sow nor reap nor gather into barns, and yet your heavenly Father feeds them. Are you not of more value than they? (Matthew 6:25–26)

Relationships

We may be able to willingly sacrifice some comfort for God without difficulty. For some of my brethren in the faith, this may come easily. For others, it may take an extra measure of prayer and faith. What if God calls us to sacrifice certain relationships? What if a friendship or even a family relationship is holding us back from our purpose in Christ? Would we be able to willingly set that aside for the greater pursuit?

I will admit I find this the most difficult. I've always been close to my family, and the few really good friends I have, whether I see them often or not, are relationships I would not want to willingly lose. But while on earth, Jesus never let relationships with others keep him from His true purpose:

> While he was still speaking to the people, behold, his mother and his brothers stood outside, asking to speak to him. But he replied to the man who told him, "Who is my mother, and who are my brothers?" And stretching out his hand toward his disciples, he said, "Here are my mother and my brothers! For whoever

does the will of my Father in heaven is my brother and sister and mother." (Mathew 12:46–50, also Mark 3:31–35)

Ministering to the crowds and teaching them about His kingdom were more important to Jesus than any specific need his family members may have had at that moment—or perhaps it is simply that He expected the same of His family as He did of the crowds. There was no favoritism simply because of familial relationships. They weren't getting the VIP passes on family name alone! Jesus does not let relational distractions keep Him from His purpose.

Similarly, some of us may be tempted to hold off on pursuits that God has placed on our hearts due to discouragement from family or friends. Even when they seem to have our best interests at heart, as Christians in pursuit of our God-given purpose, we may need to sacrifice these relationships—or the advice of these relations—to further pursue Christ.

This isn't to say we should cut off all ties with the world or those who do not believe in Christ. A friend or family member who is not a believer is not an automatic pariah to us. If anything, to a degree, we should engage more with them as we let our actions show the change Christ has made upon us. However, when the time comes to move forward in our walks, if friends or family members are hindering this, we may need to set things aside—temporarily or permanently, depending on the situation.

Again, the ultimate goal of a Christian life is fulfilling God's will and purpose for us while on earth, glorifying Him where we are able, and preaching the good news so that all who would believe can be saved. This manifests differently for different people as I've mentioned before, but what is true for all believers is that we cannot let worldly distractions—even in the form of relationships—hinder our sanctification.

A good example of a temporary sacrifice of a good relationship happened to my wife and me when we moved to Austin around 2009. My best friend had secured a job for Juliet, and I joined them in this position a month or so after the move. My friend and I hadn't spent much time together since I was in school in Oklahoma when he had moved away and began his family life. We still maintained our friendship at a distance, but hadn't spent daily time together in years.

During this absence, he had drifted completely away from Christianity while I had begun to mature in my faith. Now, we were at the same job, often in close proximity, and we began to clash a bit. I was on fire about my growth and knowledge within the faith, and he had the same fervor in his shift toward atheism. Neither of us took a respectful approach, and we found ourselves name-calling and putting one another down.

My Christian faith had become stupid to him, and although we cared about one another based on the length of our friendship, a rift began to develop. I certainly did nothing to help my case since I hadn't matured enough to fully speak to the faith I held so dearly at that time. I was somewhat obnoxious about it actually, as I recall.

It culminated—as I mentioned in "The Danger of Doubt" —with a very poorly timed article around the time of Juliet's miscarriage. We had maintained our friendship despite our occasional theological battles, but this proved it was time to give the relationship a break.

I can't recall how long it was before we tentatively began the friendship again, but I know that in the time we stopped talking, I grew more in my walk with Christ and began understanding why I believed what I believed. I was more confident yet more loving in how I spoke about it.

When the time came to explore our friendship again, we did not clash the way we had before. There was forgiveness and moving on. He hasn't changed his atheism—as far as I know—and I haven't changed my faith, but we began to be respectful of one another. We had a long talk one night while walking around his neighborhood, and I began to understand more about his turning away from the faith. These new insights to one another helped strengthen the friendship.

Now, I say this to point out that our long-lasting relationship had to be set aside temporarily for the sake of my growth in pursuit of Christ. Neither of us liked it, but the result was ultimately better. I still pray for God to work on his heart and ultimately bring him to Christ along with his family, but it is certainly not in my hands at this stage. We can hang out and visit one another when I pass through town, and his family's hospitality toward mine is always very much appreciated. They give their time and resources any time we visit.

There may be times in our Christian walks when we need to step away, temporarily or otherwise, from friends or family who would hinder our growth in pursuit of Christ. Jesus makes it apparent in His response to those saying His family wished to speak to Him that there are pursuits of greater importance than our earthly relationships. I'm not a huge fan of this because I love my family and friends, and if I had my way, I would never have to risk severing those relationships. However, I guess that God, knowing this is a weak area for me, may at some point challenge me again. And as painful as the sacrifice of relationships may be, it is a danger I willingly embrace by standing firm in the Christian faith.

For those newer to the faith who may need to adjust their surroundings a bit in terms of relationships that hinder their faith, I pray God will provide them the strength necessary to put His will over the world's concerns. Sacrificing comforts for God is certainly easier than sacrificing relationships, but the loss of friendships pales in comparison to the danger of sacrifice as it relates to giving our lives for Christ.

Giving Our Lives for Christ

I do not expect us to pursue martyrdom in Christ, and I would pray that no one experience it. But if in the future, the time comes to stand for Christ or meet Him in heaven earlier than we anticipated, I hope the Holy Spirit gives us the strength to stand firm in our faith.

Eleven of the twelve apostles died as martyrs for Christ. Only John died of old age, and even he suffered from the attempted burning by oil (based on some accounts), and was most definitely exiled away from his church home and everything he knew.[19] The willingness to sacrifice their lives when it came to standing for Christ or bowing to the world confirms what we know about the truth of the resurrection and the Bible's account, and it also confirms that an inherent danger of standing for Christ is giving our lives.

We may know we are headed to our heavenly home, but I don't know many Christians, if any, who would say they are actively trying to get there sooner. We may have confidence in our eternal life, but we don't pursue death. Some of this may be related to not understanding what awaits us after death. With so many popular misconceptions about the nature of heaven, it is no wonder that even devout Christians have trouble building hope for the life beyond.

Christ's death and resurrection stand as the foundation stones of the Christian faith, but it is easy to overlook the significance of this regarding our future state of being. Unlike the modern conception of floating on clouds and playing harps all day, we understand that our heavenly reality will, in many ways, be a perfected version of our existing reality.

Immediately upon death, we are separated from our earthly bodies, and our spirits go to be with Christ—or a place of torment for the unbeliever. However, that is not our final state. When Christ returns, Paul reminds us:

> For the Lord himself will descend from heaven with a cry of command, with the voice of an archangel, and with the sound of the trumpet of God. And the dead in Christ will rise first. Then we who are alive, who are left, will be caught up together with them in the clouds to meet the Lord in the air, and so we will always be with the Lord. (1 Thessalonians 4:16–17)

At this time, the bodies of believers who have died before Christ's return are reunited and glorified with their spirits, so that it

---

[19] Foxe, John. Foxe's Book of Martyrs, Christian Classics Ethereal Library. https://ccel.org/ccel/foxe/martyrs.

is a perfected state. Since we were created for physical dwellings, it makes sense that our heavenly bodies would retain this element of our human nature, albeit with perfection as they originally had in the garden before the fall:

> I tell you this, brothers: flesh and blood cannot inherit the kingdom of God, nor does the perishable inherit the imperishable. Behold! I tell you a mystery. We shall not all sleep, but we shall all be changed, in a moment, in the twinkling of an eye, at the last trumpet. For the trumpet will sound, and the dead will be raised imperishable, and we shall be changed. For this perishable body must put on the imperishable, and this mortal body must put on immortality. When the perishable puts on the imperishable, and the mortal puts on immortality, then shall come to pass the saying that is written: "Death is swallowed up in victory. O death, where is your victory? O death, where is your sting?" (1 Corinthians 15:50–55)

When the thief on the cross next to Christ believed, Christ promised him that on that very day, he would join Him in paradise (Luke 23:43). Paradise would be the intermediate state before the resurrection of our bodies, but it is still a place of a more temporary heavenly existence. It is something to be desired, something much better than the sin-tainted world.

For those who have died in Christ, the immediate moment after death is joyous as they enter into Christ's presence. Unlike views of a cleansing period like purgatory, mostly espoused by Roman Catholics, for the believer who has trusted in Christ for the forgiveness of their sins, there is no further payment owed to God to enter His kingdom. We are purified in His sight. He sees Christ's payment on the cross as sufficient satisfaction of our sin debt, and we enter His presence under the blood of Christ.

The idea of Christians paying for sins already forgiven at their moment of justification is a Roman Catholic Church doctrine, but it is not biblical. Since good Roman Catholics, however, believe that church tradition, scripture, and the magisterium of the church stand on equal footing, the tradition of the church can override the authority of scripture. As seen in this excerpt from the Catechism of the Catholic Church:

> It is clear therefore that, in the supremely wise arrangement of God, sacred Tradition, Sacred Scripture, and the Magisterium of the Church are so connected and associated that one of them cannot stand without the others.[20]

For any of my Roman Catholic brethren out there, just know that purgatory is part of the Catholic tradition, but it is not scriptural. If you've truly trusted in Christ for the forgiveness of your sins and rely on the authority of scripture alone—even though you are a "bad Catholic" by the Roman Catholic Church's definition—you would be a good Christian believer.

It is reassuring to know that belief in Christ and acceptance of His forgiveness are not conditioned on our ability to repay for ourselves what He already paid on our behalf on the cross. Our salvation cannot be earned because it is a gift.

Once saved, the Holy Spirit dwelling within us compels us to good works and bearing fruit. In this way, as James mentions, faith and works are intertwined—but works are a product of salvation and faith and not the means by which we attain salvation.

Since we've discussed Roman Catholicism a bit here, let's clarify one of the primary verses used by the Catholic Church to suggest that it is not faith alone that saves us. It comes from a reading of James without applying the context of the other apostles' writings on the same subject (Galatians 2:16, 3:6; Ephesians 2:8).

---

[20] Catechism of the Catholic Church, 2nd Edition. (Washington, DC: United States Catholic Conference, 2000), 29.

You see that a person is justified by works and not by faith alone. (James 2:24)

Yet we know that a person is not justified by works of the law but through faith in Jesus Christ, so we also have believed in Christ Jesus, in order to be justified by faith in Christ and not by works of the law, because by works of the law no one will be justified. (Galatians 2:16)

Just as Abraham "believed God, and it was counted to him as righteousness"? (Galatians 3:6)

For by grace you have been saved through faith. And this is not your own doing; it is the gift of God. (Ephesians 2:8)

Though Paul's writings in Galatians and Ephesians seem apparently in conflict with James 2:24, we can see that—within the context of what James is saying—faith that is merely intellectual and without any evidence of itself is dead. James even quotes what Paul had said regarding Abraham's righteousness just before verse 24. The works do not justify us anymore before God.

However, if our faith does not produce evidence of itself, is it genuine faith? R. C. Sproul stated it well in a web article written in 2018 for Ligonier Ministries:

If a person says he has faith, but he gives no outward evidence of that faith through righteous works, his faith will not justify him … We are not saved by a profession of faith or by a claim to faith. That faith has to be genuine before the merit of Christ will be imputed to anybody … True faith will absolutely and necessarily yield the fruits of obedience and the works of righteousness.[21]

Heaven, for the believer, will be a place of joy with no trace of sin or sorrow (2 Peter 3:10–13; Revelation 21:1–5; Isaiah 11:6–9, 65:17–19, 66:22; Matthew 19:28, 25:21). We will have things to do, we will be in fellowship with our Creator and other believers, and it will certainly not be a boring existence. Think of all of the things we could do without the curse of sin on this earth. Our bodies will be in peak physical condition, we will enjoy perfect fellowship with others, we will have a purpose to fulfill, and we will be with our Savior. This is the heaven of the Bible, and if we are truly in Christ, we should embrace it without fear.

Overcoming the Danger of Sacrifice

Thinking of the joys that await us in the life to come can help prepare Christians for the ultimate danger of sacrifice. Most of us, I would guess, won't become Christian martyrs. These days, in the United States, there is little risk of being killed for our faith. Perhaps there are some one-off examples, but there is certainly not persecution like Christians in the Middle East.

However, if that day comes when we are asked to deny Christ or face death, the danger of our faith is that we must face death. We must persevere to the end—even unto death. It is not something we seek, and it is not something we wish on any of our Christian brothers or sisters, but martyrdom for Christ is still a possibility when assessing the cost of following Christ.

Jesus's original followers suffered willingly, having seen the risen Christ and the promise of the resurrection. Certainly, based on some of the methods by which they were martyred, it was not

---

[21] Sproul, R.C. "Does James 2:24 Deny Justification by Faith Alone?" Ligonier Ministries. March 14, 2018, https://www.ligonier.org/blog/faith-and-works/.

anything short of torturous. However, moments later, they entered into paradise with Christ, and they now dwell with Him until He returns and establishes His kingdom on earth.

We may sacrifice creature comforts or have to give up relationships for Christ. We may even have to sacrifice our lives for Christ. The key is that sacrifice for Christ is of benefit to us. It may not seem so on the surface, but as we store up treasures in heaven and live our lives daily for Christ, anything we can give to the One who gave it all for us is of value.

I pray that we never have to die for our faith. I pray that our most important relationships have the same faith and desire for Christ. I pray that God will meet the needs of His followers. I also pray that in the absence of any one of these, we are strengthened by His Holy Spirit and propelled onward in our faith, not stepping back or denying Christ, but standing firm upon the rock.

Epilogue

WHILE READING THIS BOOK, I HOPE YOU'VE COME TO REALIZE THAT following Christ is a serious commitment that requires we count the cost. It's something we all must decide. When the Holy Spirit compels us to faith, we must not resist. We must pursue Christ and the grace and forgiveness found only in Him. Only by this may we be saved from our sins and the wrath we have stored up.

Though not all dangers will prove applicable to every single believer, I believe those discussed provide a framework of expectation. Not all of our experiences as believers will be the same, but in overcoming the dangers of following Christ and calling ourselves Christians, I believe there are key practices that apply to all.

Immersing ourselves in the Bible is the first and most effective step to overcoming the dangers inherent to a Christian life. Admittedly, it can be difficult to discipline ourselves to spend time daily in the study of the Bible. However, in my own experience, the more we dedicate to God, the more hunger for Him and His Word we will experience.

One practice I am working on in my study is to take a verse at a time and let it soak in. What did it mean then in the context of when it was written? What truths are applicable today or always? How can I apply this now? A yearly Bible reading plan can be great, but I find, for myself, I am more concerned with completion than really meditating on what I'm reading. It seems more important in overcoming the dangers of Christianity to dwell on individual passages.

Secondly, we must work on our overall relationship with God.

Beyond knowing Him and relating through His Word, we can approach Him in prayer. With Christ as our mediator, and the Holy Spirit there to take our prayers and relate them to truly express our thoughts and needs, we can speak to God personally and know He hears us. In Christ, we have access to the Father. The example before of a husband who only speaks to his wife once a week or infrequently is helpful to consider. If we are truly Christ's bride, how can we grow in a relationship with Him without speaking to Him? He hears our needs, He forgives our sins, and for the believer truly seeking His will, He works all things together ultimately for good. He is our rock when the waves crash and a firm foundation to withstand the storms of our lives.

Finally, we need fellowship with our brothers and sisters in Christ. This may be the final suggestion mentioned, but it is no less important. We cannot grow and mature in our faith without the fellowship of other believers. We need accountability and support to overcome the dangers we all face. Attending church, even at a bare minimum to have this interaction, is essential, but truly finding a church in which we can serve and in which we can connect and invest is best.

Though it has become a bit of a cliché phrase, "doing life together" is truly important within Christianity. A personal relationship with Christ does not mean we ignore all others or skip the communal gathering of believers. Sure, we can be saved and get by on sermons and messages online, but we cannot fully mature this way. And since our goal is sanctifying ourselves and becoming even more like Christ, we need this interaction with other believers.

The dangers of the Christian faith are many, yet we have the means and the tools to overcome and to achieve victory in this life as we look forward to our future heavenly existence. Christ tells us to take up our crosses and follow Him. It is a sacrifice of comfort at times, and it is not an easy life—yet the reward and fulfillment of a life lived for Christ is beyond anything the world has to offer. We may stumble in our walks, but since we are justified in the instant that we accept the Holy Spirit's call on us to faith in Christ, we can rest in our ultimate salvation from sin.

We find safety in Christ—even though a life lived for Him in our world now may come with danger. Then, as James emphasizes, our faith produces good works, and we bear fruit in this life. We can move through this life fulfilling God's purpose for us and utilizing our God-given talents. We can run the race to completion, and when it is our time, we will pass from this life to the next, ready to hear Him say, "Well done, good and faithful servant."

> If anyone comes to me and does not hate his own father and mother and wife and children and brothers and sisters, yes, and even his own life, he cannot be my disciple. Whoever does not bear his own cross and come after me cannot be my disciple. For which of you, desiring to build a tower, does not first sit down and count the cost, whether he has enough to complete it? Otherwise, when he has laid a foundation and is not able to finish, all who see it begin to mock him, saying, "This man began to build and was not able to finish." Or what king, going out to encounter another king in war, will not sit down first and deliberate whether he is able with ten thousand to meet him who comes against him with twenty thousand? And if not, while the other is yet a great way off, he sends a delegation and asks for terms of peace. So therefore, any one of you who does not renounce all that he has cannot be my disciple. (Luke 14:26–33)

Renouncing all of our earthly pleasures and treasures sounds harsh and too high of a cost—I can admit that as well as anyone—but God is looking for hearts who choose Him ultimately. His grace and mercy will catch us when we fall, and His forgiveness cleanses us of our sins. To grow and experience all God has for our lives—both here and in the world to come—we must be willing to embrace and accept what is a wonderful, relational, saving faith, but which at times is also a dangerous faith.

Becoming a Christian

Though the dangers mentioned in this book may have caused some pause, I want to assure you that Christ is with us, and His Holy Spirit guides us daily as we fight through these dangers. If you have never accepted Christ, there is no better time than now.

While we are dead in our sins, we cannot choose God (Romans 3:23–24). Only by the power of His Holy Spirit convicting and drawing us toward Him can we receive Christ in faith. We are saved by faith, not our works (Acts 15:11; Ephesians 1:7–8, 2:4–8; Galatians 3:20–24; John 1:17; Romans 3:20–24, 5:1–2, 15, 11:6; Titus 2:11; 2 Timothy 1:9).

Nothing we can do on this earth can justify us before a holy God. We are all under the penalty of sin, and without Christ, destined for God's wrath. But the good news is that God, in His infinite mercy, became like us to live the perfect life we couldn't achieve and to die the sacrificial death needed to cover our sins once and for all (Philippians 2:5–11).

Christ took this wrath on the cross. As Christ said, "It is finished." The work of redemption was completed. His resurrection days later showed that He had power over death and verified His claim to be God incarnate. In accepting Christ's call on your life and responding to his Holy Spirit's prompting on your heart, you need only do these simple things. Acknowledge that you have sinned and fallen short of God's standard, repent of your sin, and embrace the forgiveness found in a relationship with Jesus Christ. That same Holy Spirit dwells within believers, guiding us in sanctification and a life for Christ.

If you prayed for repentance and accepted Christ, you are now an adopted child of God. You are saved in that instant—though your life is to be a process of daily seeking to be like Christ. Your past habits and failures may not fall away immediately, but the Holy Spirit's conviction now will bring a desire to turn from those past behaviors and sins.

Embrace the beautiful and free gift of salvation. Though we may have dangers yet to face in this life, our heavenly home awaits one day. Every tear will be wiped away, and there will be no more pain or the effects of sin. What a blessed day that will be! Welcome to the family.

Printed in the United States
By Bookmasters